Poetry of the Spirit

Compiled, edited and with a preface
By Gerard E. Goggins

Ambassador Books
Worcester, Massachusetts

Library of Congress Catalog Card Number: 96-79064

ISBN: 0-9646439-7-9

Published by: Ambassador Books, Inc.
                 71 Elm Street
                 Worcester, MA 01609

To order, call: 800 577-0909

*This book is dedicated to
Ms. Helen Rogers,
an English teacher at Sayville High School,
in Sayville, New York
who understood the importance of poetry
and people.*

Table of Contents

ii

Preface

We are living in our own dark ages. We have lost touch with our past and with our spiritual history. We focus intently on the utilitarian, the material, and the pragmatic, and in our concern with the present and with technology, we have forgotten where we came from. One of the casualties of our near-sightedness has been poetry. Like so many of the glories of Western Civilization, it has been largely ignored.

Poetry is as old as humankind. It elevates words and gives them power. It is concise, forceful, and mysterious. It uses rhythms and sounds and meters in ways that common speech or even high rhetoric does not. It can be obscure and ambiguous, and yet, it uses those qualities to gives us revelations beyond the ability of the logical, conscious mind to grasp. The metaphors and similes poetry employs give us insights that escape dissection and analysis. In poetry we understand at a level above or below our conscious mind; we understand with something approaching our whole being – so that at its best, poetry elevates us and enlarges our vision. It speaks to the whole person and fills a human need for beauty and awe.

Many feel that today poetry is the preserve of the academic. Its power and its beauty seem to have been buried in footnotes and learned dissertations. It has been poked at and prodded, pigeon-holed and codified, and served up in survey courses to students who have seen it merely as another boring obstacle to be climbed over.

But poets have always played an essential role in society. The best are prophets. Indeed, some of the greatest prophets were among our greatest poets. We have only to think of King David whose Psalms have survived so many millenniums with no diminution in their power or their beauty, or Isaiah, or St. John who employed extraordinary poetic power in his Gospel, Letters, and Book of Revelations. It is a common misconception to believe that prophecy deals exclusively with the future. Prophets are people who examine the present and reveal its true nature. In this sense, T.S. Eliot was one of the great prophets of the Twentieth Century. He examined the malaise and the fixation with the superficial, and the anguish which that causes, with some of the most memorable poetry of our age.

This volume focuses on the spiritual nature of poetry in the religious sense. In it are poems that have been produced as poets wrestled with their consciences or with God's care. They look at love, death, nature, and self in terms of our relationship with a Being beyond our comprehension, but not beyond our reach. Here we find delight, awe and trust. Here are men and women who stand on the brink of the unknown and embrace it with a sense of impending peace and transformation.

Poetry places demands on the reader/listener that prose does not. Poetry, like music, is meant to be heard. And like music, poetry must be heard again and again before it releases all that it contains to the listener. Great music engulfs us because it overwhelms our senses – not just our sense of hearing, but our sense of touch as well, because, although we may not be aware of it, we feel the rythms, we feel the beat of the music. The sound waves impact on more than just our ear drums. Music can be thought. We can explore a written score. We can hear it in our mind, and we can recognize its beauty, its harmonies and counterpoint. But it is not the same as sitting in hall with a symphony orchestra and hearing and feeling the lushness or the astringency of the notes.

Poetry, too, can be heard in the mind. Think of Lear in the great storm scene:

Blow, winds, and crack your cheeks! Rage! Blow!
You cataracts and hurricanes, spout
Till you have drenched our steeples, drowned the cocks.
You sulphurous and thought-executing fires,
Vaunt-couriers to oak-cleaving thunderbolts,

Singe my white head! And thou, all-shaking thunder,
Smite flat the thick rotundity of the world.

(III,ii,1-6)

We hear it in our minds, but we do not hear it. Even as we read the words silently, we feel our lips moving and our chests swelling. We become animated, and we start to whisper the words – to hear their sounds and feel their dramatic force. Here is a speech that must not merely be read aloud, it must be read forcefully. And when we speak it out, we feel its power and emotion. We become Lear. We identify with his anguish.

Poetry is the most intimate of communications, but it dies, or at least it suffers, in silence. Can you imagine if we could only read the great choruses of Bach and Handel or only read Beethoven's symphonies and Mozart's piano concertos?

Poetry demands sound because it is built on sound as much as music is.

Poetry demands passion, because poetry is passionate. Poetry must be read aloud and with passion if it is to reveal to us its depths.

The poems in this volume are both beautiful and passionate. They represent great variety. We have William Blake asking:

Little lamb who made thee?
Dost thou know who made thee?

And John Donne visualizing the end of the world:

At the round Earth's imagined corners, blow
Your trumpets angels, and arise, arise
From death, you numberless infinities

Gerard Manley Hopkins using metrics and rhythms to describe the soaring flight of a falcon:

I caught this morning morning's minion,
 kingdom of daylight's dauphin,
 dapple-dawn-drawn
Falcon in his riding
Of the rolling level underneath him steady air,
 and striding
High there, how he rung upon the rein
 of a wimpling wing
In his ecstasy! Then off, off forth on swing. . .

Yes, Hopkins can be difficult. Men do not dig mines because gold is easily accessible. Poetry makes demands on us. Good poetry is not for everyone. Although it should be, it never has been, because poetry requires patience and involvement. We must enter the poem and then surrender to it.

There is something else going on in these poems besides good poetry. This is poetry that is concerned with the higher things. It searches and examines and reflects; it probes and explores and attempts to comprehend the meaning and nature of our relationship with God. This is noble poetry which celebrates life in its mystery, its pain, and its joy.

--Gerard E. Goggins

William Blake

1757-1827

William Blake was a man with a very personal vision. He was and remains outside the mainstream of English poetry. He was not born into the ruling class nor was he a gentleman with ties to Cambridge or Oxford. He was a tradesman, a printer and engraver.

But he was a man with a pure and powerful poetic vision; indeed, he was something of a mystic. He had his first vision of angels when he was about eight years old. Thereafter, he was filled with certainty that God is kind and tender and loving and that creation is filled with wonder and delight.

It is impossible to read Blake's poetry and not realize that he had a special relationship with and understanding of his maker. Indeed, his wife once said, "I have very little of Mr. Blake's company. He is always in Paradise."

The Divine Image

To Mercy, Pity, Peace, and Love,
All pray in their distress:
And to these virtues of delight
Return their thankfulness.

For Mercy, Pity, Peace, and Love,
Is God our father dear:
And Mercy, Pity, Peace, and Love,
Is Man, his child and care.

For Mercy has a human heart
Pity, a human face:
And Love, the human form divine,
And Peace, the human dress.

Then every man of every clime,
That prays in his distress,
Prays to the human form divine
Love, Mercy, Pity, Peace.

And all must love the human form,
In heathen, Turk or Jew.
Where Mercy, Love and Pity dwell
There God is dwelling too.

A Cradle Song

Sweet dreams form a shade,
Over my lovely infant's head.
Sweet dreams of pleasant streams.
By happy, silent, moony, beams.

Sweet sleep, with soft down,
Weave thy brows an infant crown.
Sweet sleep, Angel mild,
Hover over my happy child.

Sweet smiles in the night,
Hover over my delight.
Sweet smiles, Mothers smiles,
All the livelong night beguiles.

Sweet moans, dove-like sighs,
Chase not slumber from thy eyes.
Sweet moans, sweeter smiles.
All the dove-like moans beguiles.

Sleep, sleep, happy child.
All creation slept and smiled.
Sleep, sleep, happy sleep.
While over thee thy mother weeps.

Sweet babe in thy face,
Holy image I can trace.
Sweet babe once like thee,
Thy maker lay and wept for me,

Wept for me, for thee, for all,
When he was an infant small.
Thou his image ever see.
Heavenly face that smiles on thee.

Smiles on thee, on me, on all,
Who became an infant small,
Infant smiles are his own smiles.
Heaven and earth to peace beguiles.

Another's Sorrow

Can I see another's woe,
And not be in sorrow too?
Can I see another's grief,
And not seek for kind relief?

Can I see a falling tear,
And not feel my sorrows share?
Can a father see his child,
Weep, nor be with sorrow filled?

Can a mother sit and hear,
An infant groan? an infant fear?
No, no, never can it be.
Never, never can it be.

And can he who smiles on all,
Hear the wren with sorrows small,
Hear the small birds grief and care
Hear the woes that infants bear —

And not sit beside the nest,
Pouring pity in their breast?
And not sit the cradle near,
Weeping tear on infants tear?

And not sit both night and day,
Wiping all our tears away?
O! no, never can it be.
Never, never can it be.

He doth give his joy to all.
He becomes an infant small.
He becomes a man of woe.
He doth feel the sorrow too.

The Lamb

Little Lamb who made thee?
Dost thou know who made thee?
Gave thee life and bid thee feed
By the stream and o'er the mead:
Gave thee clothing of delight,
Softest clothing, wooly, bright;
Gave thee such a tender voice,
Making all the vales rejoice?
Little Lamb who made thee
Dost thou know who made thee?

Little Lamb I'll tell thee,
Little Lamb I'll tell thee:
He is called by thy name,
For he calls himself a Lamb.
He is meek and he is mild,
He became a little child.
I a child and thou a lamb;
We are called by his name.
Little Lamb God bless thee!
Little Lamb God bless thee!

The Tiger

Tiger, Tiger, burning bright,
In the forests of the night:
What immortal hand or eye,
Could frame thy fearful symmetry?

In what distant deeps or skies
Burnt the fire of thine eyes?
On what wings dare he aspire?
What the hand, dare seize the fire?

And what shoulder, and what art,
Could twist the sinews of thy heart?
And when thy heart began to beat,
What dread hand? and what dread feet?

What the hammer? what the chain,
In what furnace was thy brain?
What the anvil? what dread grasp,
Dare its deadly terrors clasp?

When the stars threw down their spears,
And watered heaven with their tears:
Did He smile his work to see?
Did He who made the Lamb make thee?

Night

The sun descending in the west,
The evening star does shine.
The birds are silent in their nest,
And I must seek for mine.
The moon like a flower,
In heavens high bower;
With silent delight,
Sits and smiles on the night.

Farewell green fields and happy groves,
Where flocks have took delight;
Where lambs have nibbled, silent moves
The feet of angels bright;
Unseen they pour blessing,
And joy without ceasing,
On each bud and blossom,
And each sleeping bosom.

They look in every thoughtless nest,
Where birds are covered warm;
They visit caves of every beast,
To keep them all from harm;
If they see any weeping,
That should have been sleeping,
They pour sleep on their head
And sit down by their bed.
When wolves and tigers howl for prey,

They pitying stand and weep;
Seeking to drive their thirst away,
And keep them from the sheep.
But if they rush dreadful;
The angels most heedful,
Receive each mild spirit,
New worlds to inherit.

And there the lion's ruddy eyes,
Shall flow with tears of gold:
And pitying the tender cries,
And walking round the fold:
Saying: wrath by his meekness
And by his health, sickness,
Is driven away,
From our immortal day.

And now beside thee bleating lamb,
I can lie down and sleep;
Or think on him who bore thy name,
Graze after thee and weep.
For washed in life's river,
My bright mane forever,
Shall shine like the gold,
As I guard o'er the fold.

The Shepherd

How sweet is the Shepherd's sweet lot,
From the morn to the evening he strays:
He shall follow his sheep all the day
And his tongue shall be filled with praise.

For he hears the lamb's innocent call.
And he hears the ewes tender reply.
He is watchful while they are in peace.
For they know when their Shepherd is nigh.

Holy Thursday

'Twas on a Holy Thursday, their innocent faces clean,
The children walking two and two,
    in red and blue and green.
Grey headed beadles walked before with wands
    as white as snow,
Till into the high dome of Paul's, they like Thames
    waters flow.

O what a multitude they seemed, these flowers
    of London town,
Seated in companies, they sit with radiance all their own.
The hum of multitudes was there, but multitudes
    of lambs,
Thousands of little boys and girls raising
    their innocent hands.

Now like a mighty wind, they raise to heaven
    the voice of song,
Or like harmonious thunderings,
    the seats of heaven among.
Beneath them sit the aged men, wise guardians
    of the poor.
Then cherish pity, lest you drive an angel from your door.

Holy Thursday

Is this a holy thing to see,
In a rich and fruitful land,
Babes reduced to misery,
Fed with cold and usurious hand?

Is that trembling cry a song?
Can it be a song of joy?
And so many children poor?
It is a land of poverty!

And their sun does never shine.
And their fields are bleak and bare.
And their ways are filled with thorns.
It is eternal winter there.

For where-ever the sun does shine,
And where-ever the rain does fall:
Babe can never hunger there,
Nor poverty the mind appall.

Emily Bronte

1818-1848

Emily Bronte longed to be her own woman, to be free in ways women could not be in 19th Century England. She was never able to escape the economic and social restraints placed upon her by virtue of her gender.

Even so her brilliant talent was not to be denied. With Wuthering Heights, she made her mark as one of the great English novelists.

The two poems presented here, show a spiritual progression as her focus moves from self and anguish to trust and fulfillment.

Often Rebuked, Yet Always Back Returning

Often rebuked, yet always back returning
    To those first feelings that were born with me,
And leaving busy chase of wealth and learning
    For idle dreams of things which cannot be:

Today, I will seek not the shadowy region;
    Its unsustaining vastness waxes drear;
And visions rising, legion after legion,
    Bring the unreal world too strangely near.

I'll walk, but not in old heroic traces,
    And not in paths of high morality,
and not among the half-distinguished faces,
    The clouded forms of long-past history.

I'll walk where my own nature would be leading—
    It vexes me to choose another guide—
Where the gray flocks in ferny glens are feeding,
    Where the wild wind blows on the mountain-side.

What have those lonely mountains worth revealing?
More glory and more grief than I can tell:
The earth that wakes one human heart to feeling
Can center both the worlds of Heaven and Hell.

No Coward Soul Is Mine

These are the last lines Emily Bronte ever wrote

No coward soul is mine,
No trembler in the world's storm-troubled sphere;
I see Heaven's glories shine,
And faith shines equal, arming me from fear.

O God within my breast,
Almighty, ever-present Deity!
Life—that in me has rest,
As I—undying Life—have power in Thee.

Vain are the thousand creeds
That move men's hearts unutterably vain;
Worthless as withered weeds,
Or idlest froth amid the boundless main,

To waken doubt in one
Holding so fast by Thine infinity;
So surely anchored on
The steadfast rock of immortality.

With wide-embracing love
Thy spirit animates eternal years,
Pervades and broods above,
Changes, sustains, dissolves, creates, and rears.

Though earth and man were gone,
And suns and universes ceased to be,
And Thou were left alone,
Every existence would exist in Thee.

There is not room for Death,
Nor atom that his might could render void;
Thou—Thou art Being and Breath,
And what Thou art may never by destroyed.

William Cowper

1731-1800

William Cowper suffered great spiritual torment for most of his life. He was the victim of a melancholy disorder which led him to attempt suicide three times. He was befriended by the Unwins, a clergyman and his wife, with whom he lived for many years. Cowper believed that he had committed unpardonable sin and that he was destined to spend eternity in hell. Even so, he devoted part of his life to parish work. He also wrote the Olney Hymns, more than eighty in number, which became famous. However, his bouts of insanity got progressively worse. When Mrs. Unwin died in 1796, his insanity returned and remained with him until the end of his life.

Walking With God

Oh! for a closer walk with God,
A calm and heavenly frame,
A light to shine upon the road
That leads me to the Lamb!

Where is the blessedness I knew
When first I saw the Lord?
Where is the soul-refreshing view
Of Jesus and his word?

What peaceful hours I once enjoyed!
How sweet their memory still!
But they have left an aching void
The world can never fill.

Return, O holy Dove, return,
Sweet messenger of rest!
I hate the sins that made Thee mourn,
And drove Thee from my breast.

The dearest idol I have known,
Whatever that idol be,
Help me to tear it from Thy throne,
and worship only Thee.

So shall my walk be close with God,
Calm and serene my frame;
So purer light shall mark the road
That leads me to the Lamb.

Praise for the Fountain Opened

There is a fountain filled with blood
Drawn from Emmanuel's veins;
And sinners, plunged beneath that flood,
Lose all their guilty stains.

The dying thief rejoiced to see
That fountain in his day;
And there have I, as vile as he,
Washed all my sins away.

Dear dying Lamb, Thy precious blood
Shall never lose its power,
Till all the ransomed Church of God
Be saved to sin no more.

Ever since, by faith, I saw the stream
Thy flowing wounds supply,
Redeeming love has been my theme,
And shall be till I die.

Then in a nobler, sweeter song,
I'll sing Thy power to save;
When this poor lisping stammering tongue
Lies silent in the grave.

Look, I believe Thou hast prepared
(unworthy though I be)
For me a blood-bought free reward,
A golden harp for me!

'Tis strung, and tuned, for endless years,
And formed by power divine,
To sound in God the Father's ears
No other name but Thine.

Emily Dickinson

1830-1896

Emily Dickinson was a genius who labored in obscurity. She was born and lived a reclusive life in Amherst, Massachusetts. In 1862, she sent four poems to Thomas Wentworth Higginson, a man of letters. He rejected the poems but continued to correspond with Miss Dickinson. Higginson saw Miss Dickinson only twice although they corresponded for many years.

After Miss Dickinson died in 1896, her sister Lavinia found a box containing hundreds of her poems. Higginson helped to prepare them for publication.

LX

The Soul's Storm

It struck me every day
The lightning was as new
As if the cloud that instant slit
    And let the fire through.

It burned me in the night,
    It blistered in my dream;
It sickened fresh upon my sight
    With every morning's beam.

I thought that storm was brief,—
    The maddest, quickest by;
But Nature lost the date of this,
    And left it in the sky.

LVI

Far from love the Heavenly Father
    Leads the chosen child;
Oftener through realm of briar
    Than the meadow mild,

Oftener by the claw of dragon
    Than the hand of friend,
Guides the little one predestined
    To the native land.

CXXVII

I never saw a moor,
I never saw the sea;
Yet know I how the heather looks,
And what a wave must be.

I never spoke with God,
Nor visited in heaven;
Yet certain am I of the spot
As if the chart were given.

CXXIX

I shall know why, when time is over,
And I have ceased to wonder why;
Christ will explain each separate anguish
in the fair schoolroom of the sky.

He will tell me what Peter promised,
And I, for wonder at his woe,
I shall forget the drop of anguish
That scalds me now, that scalds me now.

CIII

At least to pray is left, is left.
O Jesus! in the air
I know not which thy chamber is,—
I'm knocking everywhere.

Thou stirrest earthquake in the South,
And maelstrom in the sea;
Say, Jesus Christ of Nazareth,
Hast thou no arm for me?

LXIV

Epitaph

Step lightly on this narrow spot!
The broadest land that grows
Is not so ample as the breast
These emerald seams enclose.

Step lofty; for this name is told
As far as cannon dwell,
Or flag subsist, or fame export
Her deathless syllable.

CXLI

Farewell

Tie the strings to my life, my Lord,
  Then I am ready to go!
Just a look at the horses –
  Rapid! That will do!

Put me in on the firmest side,
  So I shall never fall;
For we must ride to the Judgment,
  And it's partly down hill.

But never I mind the bridges,
  And never I mind the sea;
Held fast in everlasting race
  By my own choice and thee.

Good-by to the life I used to live,
  And the world I used to know;
And kiss the hills for me, just once;
  Now I am ready to go!

John Donne

1571-1631

John Donne ranks among the greatest poets who have written in English. His ability to fuse experience with intellect in a disciplined but highly poetic form made him the greatest of the Metaphyscial Poets. Donne, however, transcends schools and labels. His poetic voice is unique and powerful. It also charts the spiritual journey of a man, who when he was young, showed great interest in the flesh and in the world, and was disappointed in love. But like Augustine, Donne ultimately entered religious life. As dean of St. Paul's Cathedral in London, he became a noted preacher. His later poetry reveals a very deep and trusting relationship with God. His prose meditations have a profound spirituality and are highly poetic in themselves. Meditation 17 has been included here.

Sonnet 7

At the round earth's imagined corners, blow
Your trumpets, Angels, and arise, arise
From death, you numberless infinities
Of souls, and to your scattered bodies go
All whom the flood did, and fire shall overthrow,
All whom war, dearth, age, agues, tyrannies,
Despair, law, chance, have slain, and you whose eyes,
Shall behold God, and never taste death's woe.
But let them sleep, Lord, and me mourn a space,
For, if above all these, my sins abound,
It's late to ask abundance of your grace,
When we are there; here on this lowly ground,
Teach me how to repent; for that's as good
As if you had sealed my pardon, with your blood.

Sonnet 10

Death be not proud, though some have called you
Mighty and dreadful, for, you are not so,
For, those, whom you think, you overthrow,
Die not, poor death, nor yet can you kill me.
From rest and sleep, which but your pictures be,
Much pleasure, then from you, much more must flow,
And soonest our best men do with you go,
Rest of their bones, and souls delivery.
You are slave to Fate, Chance, kings, and desperate men,
And do with poison, war, and sickness dwell,
And poppy, or charms can make us sleep as well,
And better than your stroke; why then do you swell?
One short sleep past, we wake eternally,
And death shall be no more; death, you shall die

Meditation 17

Perchance he for whom this bell tolls, may be so ill, that he knows not it tolls for him; And perchance I think myself so much better than I am, as that they who are about me, and see my state, may have caused it to toll for me, and I know not that.

The Church is Catholic, universal, so are all her actions; all that she does, belongs to all. When she baptizes a child, that action concerns me for that child is thereby connected to that Head which is my Head too, and engrafted into that body, whereof I am a member. And when she buries a man, that action concerns me. All mankind is of one Author, and is one volume; when man dies, one chapter is not torn out of the book, but translated into a better language; and every chapter must be translated -- God employs several translators; some pieces translated by age, some by sickness, some by war, some justice; but God's hand is in every translation; and his hand shall bind up all our scattered leaves again, for that library where every book shall lie open to one another: therefore the bell that rings to a sermon, calls not upon the preacher only, but upon the congregation to come; so the bell calls us all: but how much more me, who am brought so near the door by this sickness.

There was a contention as far as a suit, (in which both piety and dignity, religion and estimation, were mingled) which of the religious orders should ring to prayers first in the morning; and it was determined, that they should ring first that rose earliest. If we understand aright the dignity of this bell that tolls for evening prayer, we would be glad to make it ours, by rising early, in that application, that it might be ours, as well as his, whose indeed it is. The bell doth toll for him that thinks it doth; and though it intermit again, yet from that minute that occasion wrought upon him, he is united to God. Who casts not up his eye to the sun when it rises? But who takes off his eye from a comet when that breaks out? Who bends not his ear to any bell, which upon any occasion rings? But who can remove it from that bell, which is passing a piece of himself out of this world?

No man is an island entire of itself, every man is a piece of the Continent, a part of the main; if a clod be washed away by the sea Europe is the less, as well as if a promontory were, as well if a manor of thy friend's or of thine own were; any man's death diminishes me, because I am involved in mankind; And therefore never send to know for whom the bells; It tolls for thee.

Neither can we call this a begging of misery or a borrowing of Misery, as though we were not miserable enough of ourselves, but must fetch in more from the next house, in taking upon us the misery of our neighbors. Truly it were an excusable covetousness if we did for affliction is a treasure, and scarce any man hath enough it. No man hath affliction enough that is not matured, and ripened by it, and made fit for God by that affliction. If a man carry treasure in bullion, or in a wedge of gold, and have none coined into current money, his treasure will not defray him as he travels. Tribulation is treasure in the nature of it, but it is not current money in the use of it, except we get nearer and nearer our home, Heaven, by it. Another man may be sick too, and sick to death, and this affliction may in his bowels, as gold in a mine, and be of no use to him; this bell, that tells me of his affliction, digs out, and applies gold to me; if by this consideration of another's danger, I take mine own into contemplation, and so secure myself, making my recourse to my God, who is our only security.

A Hymn to God the Father

Will You forgive that sin where I begun,
Which is my sin, though it were done before?
Will You forgive that sin through which I run,
And do run still, though still I do deplore?
  When You have done, You have not done,
      For I have more.

Will You forgive that sin by which I have won
Others to sin? and made my sin their door?
Will You forgive that sin which I did shun
A year, or two, but wallowed in a score?
  When You have done, You have not done,
      For I have more.

I have a sin of fear, that when I have spun
My last thread, I shall perish on the shore;
Swear by Thyself, that at my death Thy Son
Shall shine as He shines now, and heretofore;
  And, having done that, You have done,
      I fear no more.

Michael Drayton

1563-1631

Michael Drayton had an inauspicious beginning as a poet. His first work, The Harmony of the Church, was ordered burned by the Archbishop of Canterbury. Later poems were better received and Drayton was a very popular poet in his lifetime. In his day, poets often had to rely on patrons At one point, Drayton had to turn to hack writing for the stage. Yet, he maintained a reputation as a man of virtue.

The Song of Jonah in the Whale's Belly

In the second chapter of Jonah

In grief and anguish of my heart my voice I did extend
Unto the Lord, and he thereto a willing ear did lend;
Even from the deep and darkest pit and the infernal lake
To me he hath bowed down his ear
     for his great mercy's sake.
For thou into the midst of surging seas so deep
Hast cast me forth, whose bottom is so low
     and wondrous steep,
Whose mighty wallowing waves,
     which from the floods do flow,
Have with their power up swallowed me
     and overwhelmed me tho.
Then said I, "Lo, I am exiled from presence of thy face,
Yet will I once again behold thy house and dwelling place.
The waters have encompassed me, the floods
     enclosed me round,
The weeds have sore encumbered me
     which in the seas abound.
Unto the valleys down I went, beneath the hills which stand,
The earth hath there environed me with force of all the land.
Yet hast thou still preserved me from all these dangers here
And brought my life out of the pit, O Lord my God so dear."
My soul consuming thus with care, I prayed unto the Lord,
And he from out his holy place heard me with one accord.
Who to vain lying vanities doth wholly him betake
Doth err also; God's mercy he doth utterly forsake.
But I will offer unto him the sacrifice of praise,
And pay my vows, ascribing thanks unto the Lord always.

Fulke Greville

1554-1628

Fulke Greville ranks among the Metaphysical Poets. He was a friend of Sir Philip Sidney, and was indeed so proud of their relationship, that it is recorded in his epitaph. Most of his poetry was not published until after his death, which occurred at the hands of a servant who was disappointed by the provisions of Greville's will.

Sonnet 110

Zion lies waste, and thy Jerusalem,
O Lord, is fallen to utter desolation;
Against thy prophets and thy holy men
The sin hath wrought a fatal combination;
Profaned thy name, thy worship overthrown,
And made thee, living Lord, a God unknown.

Thy powerful laws, thy wonders of creation,
Thy Word incarnate, glorious heaven, dark hell,
Lie shadowed under mall's degeneration;
Thy Christ still crucified for doing well;
Impiety, O Lord, sits on thy throne,
Which makes thee, living light, a God unknown.

Man's superstition hath thy truths entombed,
His atheism again her pomps defaces;
That sensual unsatiable vast womb
Of thy seen church thy unseen church disgraces.
There lives no truth with them that seem thine own,
Which makes thee, living Lord, a God unknown.

Yet unto thee, Lord, mirror of transgression,
We who for earthly idols have forsaken
Thy heavenly image, sinless, pure impression,
And so in nets of vanity lie taken,
All desolate implore that to thine own,
Lord, thou no longer live a God unknown.

Yet, Lord, let Israel's plagues not be eternal,
Nor sin forever cloud thy sacred mountains,
Nor with false flames, spiritual but infernal,
Dry up thy mercy's ever-springing fountains.
Rather, sweet Jesus, fill up time and come
To yield the sin her everlasting doom.

George Herbert

1593-1633

George Herbert was made Public Orator of Cambridge in 1619, when he was twenty-six. The position brought him into contact with the rich and powerful and even the king. He seemed destined for a career at court until he suffered a serious illness at about the time his mother, the king and several friends died. He resigned the oratorship and was ordained. He became rector of one of the smallest churches in England where he led a saintly life. As he lay dying, he sent his poetry to a friend to be published if the friend thought the poems would help others or to be burnt if the poetry was unworthy. The poems were printed and went through many editions.

Mortification

How soon doth man decay!
When clothes are taken from a chest of sweets
To swaddle infants, whose young breath
Scarce knows the way;
Those cloths are little winding sheets
Which do consign and send them unto death.

When boys go first to bed,
They step into their voluntary graves,
Sleep binds them fast; only their breath
Makes them not dead:
Successive nights, like rolling waves,
Convey them quickly, who are bound for death.

When youth is frank and free,
And calls for music, while his veins do swell,
All day exchanging mirth and breath
In company;
That music summons to the knell,
Which shall befriend him at the hour of death.

When man grows staid and wise,
Getting a house and home, where he may move
Within the circle of his breath,
Schooling his eyes;
That dumb inclosure makes love
Unto the coffin that attends his death.

When age grows low and weak,
Marking his grave, and thawing every year,
Till all do melt, and drown his breath
When he would speak;

A chair or litter shows the bier,
Which shall convey him to the house of death.

Man, ere he is aware,
Hath put together a solemnity,
And dressed his hearse, while he has breath
As yet to spare:
Yet Lord, instruct us so to die,
That all these dyings may be life in death.

Man

My God, I heard this day,
That none does build a stately habitation,
But he that means to dwell therein.
What house more stately has there been,
Or can be, than is Man? to whose creation
All things are in decay,

For Man is everything,
And more: He is a tree, yet bears more fruit;
A beast, yet is, or should be more:
Reason and speech we only bring.
Parrots may thank us, if they are not mute,
They go upon the score.

Man is all symmetry,
Full of proportions, one limb to another,
And all to all the world besides:
Each part may call the furthest, brother:
For head with foot hath private amity,
And both with moons and tides.

Nothing hath got so far,
But Man hath caught and kept it, as his prey.
His eyes dismount the highest star:
He is in little all the sphere.
Herbs gladly cure our flesh; because that they
Find their acquaintance there.

For us the winds do blow,
The earth doth rest, heaven move,
and fountains flow.
Nothing we see, but means our good,

As our delight, or as our treasure:
The whole is, either our cupboard of food,
    Or cabinet of pleasure.

    The stars have us to bed;
Night draws the curtain,
        which the sun withdraws;
    Music and light attend our head.
All things unto our flesh are kind
    In their descent and being; to our mind
In their ascent and cause.

    Each thing is full of duty:
Waters united are our navigation;
    Distinguished, our habitation;
Below, our drink; above, our meat;
    Both are our cleanliness. Hath one such beauty?
Then how are all things neat?

    More servants wait on Man,
Than he'll take notice of: in every path
    He treads down that which doth befriend him,
When sickness makes him pale and wan.
    Oh mighty love ! Man is one world, and hath
Another to attend him.

    Since then, my God, thou hast
So brave a Palace built; O dwell in it,
    That it may dwell with thee at last !
Till then, afford us so much wit;
    That, as the world serves us, we may sen
And both thy servants be.

The Temper

How should I praise thee, Lord!
How should my rhymes
Gladly engrave thy love in steel,
If what my soul doth feel sometimes,
My soul might ever feel!

Although there were some forty heavens, or more,
Sometimes I peer above them all;
Sometimes I hardly reach a score,
Sometimes to hell I fall.

O rack me not to such a vast extent;
Those distances belong to thee:
The world's too little for thy tent,
A grave too big for me.

Wilt thou meet arms with man, that thou dost stretch
A crumb of dust from heaven to hell?

Will great God measure with a wretch?
Shall he thy stature spell?

O let me, when thy roof my soul hath hid,
O let me roost and nestle there:
Then of a sinner thou art rid,
And I of hope and fear.

Yet take thy way; for sure thy way is best:
Stretch or contract me, thy poor debtor:
This is but tuning of my breast,
To make the music better.

Whether I fly with angels, fall with dust,
Thy hands made both, and I am there:
Thy power and love, my love and trust
Make one place every where.

The Agony

Philosophers have measured mountains,
Fathomed the depths of seas,
      of states, and kings,
Walked with a staff to heaven,
      and traced fountains:
But there are two vast, spacious things,
The which to measure it doth more behove:
Yet few there are that sound them; Sin and Love.

Who would know Sin, let him repair
Unto Mount Olive; there shall he see
A man so wrung with pains, that all his hair,
His skin, his garments bloody be.
Sin is that press and vice, which forces pain
To hunt his cruel food through every vein.

Who knows not Love, let him assay
And taste that juice, which on the cross a pike
Did see again abroach; then let him say
If ever he did taste the like.
Love is that liquor sweet and most divine,
Which my God feels as blood; but I, as wine.

Prayer

Prayer the Church's banquet, Angels age,
Gods breath in man returning to his birth,
The soul in paraphrase, heart in pilgrimage,
The Christian plummet sounding heaven
      and earth;
Engine against the Almighty, sinners tower,
Reversed thunder, Christ-side-piercing spear,
The six days world transposing in an hour,
A kind of tune, which all things hear and fear;
Softness, and peace, and joy, and love, and bliss,
Exalted Manna, gladness of the best,
Heaven in ordinary, man well dressed,
The milky way, the bird of Paradise,
Church bells beyond the stars heard,
      the soul's blood,
The land of spices; something understood.

Gerard Manley Hopkins

1844-1889

Gerard Manley Hopkins joined the Jesuits in 1868 and was ordained a priest in 1877. For a time he served in working-class parishes in Liverpool, and, then, in 1884 he was appointed Professor of Classics at University College in Dublin. If we knew him only through his poetry, we would recognize him as a deeply spiritual man who at times seems engaged in almost cosmic battle. To some, his poetry may seem difficult or inaccessible, but Hopkins can reach the highest order, indeed there are times when his poetry almost leaves words behind and becomes only sounds and rhythms and motion. All of his poetry was published posthumously, and the first edition did not come out until 1918 – twenty-nine years after his death.

Spring and Fall
To a Young Child

Margaret, are you grieving
Over Goldengrove unleaving?
Leaves, like the things of man, you
With your fresh thoughts care for, can you?
Ah! as the heart grows older
It will come to such sights colder
By and by, nor spare a sigh
Though worlds of wanwood leafmeal lie
And yet you will weep and know why.
Now no matter, child, the name:
Sorrow's springs are the same.
Nor mouth had, no nor mind, expressed
What heart heard of, ghost guessed:
It is the blight man was born for,
It is Margaret you mourn for.

God's Grandeur

The world is charged with the grandeur of God.
It will flame out, like shining from shook foil;
It gathers to a greatness, like the ooze of oil
Crushed. Why do men then now not reck his rod?
Generations have trod, have trod, have trod;
And all is smeared with trade; bleared, smeared with toil;
And wears man's smudge and shares man's smell: the soil
Is bare now, nor can foot feel, being shod.

And for all this, nature is never spent;
There lives the dearest freshness deep down things;
And though the last lights off the black West went,
Oh, morning at the brown brink eastward, springs—
Because the Holy Ghost over the bent
World broods with warm breast and with ah! bright wings.

Pied Beauty

Glory be to God for dappled things—
For skies of couple-color as a brinded cow;
For rose-moles all in stipple upon trout
        that swim;
Fresh-firecoal chestnut-falls; finches' wings;
Landscape plotted and pieced—
        fold, fallow, and plow;
And all trades, their gear and tackle and trim.

All things counter, original, spare, strange;
Whatever is fickle, freckled (who knows how?)
With swift, slow; sweet, sour; adazzle, dim;
He fathers-forth whose beauty is past change:
        Praise him.

The Windhover

To Christ Our Lord

I caught this morning morning's minion,
        kingdom of the daylight's dauphin,
        dapple-dawn-drawn Falcon, in his riding
Of the rolling level underneath him steady air,
        and striding
High there, how he rung upon the rein
        of a wimpling wing
In his ecstasy! then off, off forth on a swing,
    As a skate's heel sweeps smooth on a bow-bend—
        the hurl and gliding
    Rebuffed the big wind. My heart in hiding
Stirred for a bird—the achieve of, the mastery of the thing!

Brute beauty and valor and act, oh, air, pride, plume, here
    Buckle! and the fire that breaks from thee then, a billion
Times told lovelier, more dangerous, O my chevalier!

    No wonder of it: sheer plod makes plow down sillion
Shine, and blue-bleak embers, ah, my dear,
    Fall, gall themselves, and gash gold-vermillion.

Thou Art Indeed Just, Lord

Justus quidem tu es, Domine, si disputem tecum, verumta-
men justa loquar ad te: Quare via impiorum prosperatur?
etc.

Thou art indeed just, Lord, if I contend
With thee, but, sir, so what I plead is just.
Why do sinners' ways prosper? and why must
Disappointment all I endeavour end?
Wert thou my enemy, O thou my friend,
How wouldst thou worse, I wonder, than thou dost
Defeat, thwart me? Oh, the sots and thralls of lust
Do in spare hours more thrive than I that spend,
Sir, life upon thy cause. See, banks and brakes
Now, leaved how thick! laced they are again
With fretty chervil, look, and fresh wind shakes
Them, birds build—but not I build; no, but strain,
Time's eunuch, and not breed one work that wakes.
Mine, O thou lord of life, send my roots rain.

Heaven—Haven

(A Nun Takes the Veil)

I have desired to go
Where springs not fail
To fields where flies no sharp and sided hail
And a few lilies blow.

And I have asked to be
Where no storms come
Where the green swell is in the haven dumb,
And out of the swing of the sea.

Ben Jonson

1573–1637

Ben Jonson came from humble origins. His father, a minister, died when Ben was a young boy. His mother married a bricklayer, and Ben may have followed that trade for a while. There is no record of him having attended Oxford or Cambridge, but he became classicist of the first rank. In an age of great dramatists, including Shakespeare and Marlowe, he ranked among the best. In 1616, the year Shakespeare died, Jonson was appointed court poet. Hymn to God the Father was written late in his life.

Hymn to God the Father

Hear me, O God!
A broken heart,
Is my best part:
Use still thy rod
That I may prove
Therein, thy Love.

If thou hadst not
Been stern to me
But left me free,
I had forgot
My self and thee.

For, sin's so sweet,
As minds ill bent
Rarely repent
Until they meet
Their punishment.

Who more can crave
Than thou hast done?
That gave a Son
To free a slave,
First made of nought-
With all since bought.

Sin, Death, and Hell
His glorious Name
Quite overcame,
Yet I rebel,
And slight the same.

But, I'll come in,
Before my loss
Me farther toss,
As sure to win
Under his Cross.

John Milton

1608-1674

John Milton was a man of genius and contradiction. He was vain, difficult to live with and, perhaps, something of a misogynist. He was also a man of strong religious and political convictions. His prose is often as vitriolic and mean as his poetry is beautiful and sublime.

Milton was both a Puritan and puritanical. He was a supporter of Oliver Cromwell and received a government position during the revolution in England. He wrote in support of the right of Parliament to put the king to death. That happened in 1649 when Charles I was executed.

The monarchy was eventually restored, but Charles II did not take vengeance on the poet. And it was during the Restoration that Milton produced his greatest work, Paradise Lost. It was a mark of Milton's pride and his ambition that he announced that the purpose of his great work was to "justify the ways of God to men."

Sonnet VII

How Soon Hath Time

How soon hath Time, the subtle thief of youth,
Stolen on his wing my three and twentieth year!
My hasting days fly on with full career,
But my late spring no bud or blossom showeth.
Perhaps my semblance might deceive the truth,
That I to manhood am arrived so near,
And inward ripeness doth much less appear,
That some more timely-happy spirits endu'th.
Yet be it less or more, or soon or slow,
It shall be still in strictest measure even
To that same lot, however mean or high,
Toward which Time leads me, and the will of Heaven;
All is, if I have grace to use it so,
As ever in my great task-Master's eye.

On Time

Fly envious Time, till thou run out thy race,
Call on the lazy leaden-stepping hours,
Whose speed is but the heavy Plummet's pace;
And glut thyself with what thy womb devours,
Which is no more than what is false and vain,
And merely mortal dross;
So little is our loss,
So little is thy gain.
For when as each thing bad thou has entombed,
And, last of all, thy greedy self consumed,
Then long Eternity shall greet our bliss
With an individual kiss;
And Joy shall overtake us as a flood,
When everything that is sincerely good
And perfectly divine,
With Truth, and Peace, and Love, shall ever shine
About the supreme Throne
Of him, to whose happy-making sight alone,
When once our heavenly-guided soul shall climb,
Then all this Earthy grossness quit,
Attired with Stars, we shall for ever sit,
Triumphing over death, and Chance, and thee
  O Time.

At a Solemn Music

Blest pair of Sirens, pledges of Heaven's joy,
Sphere-born harmonious sisters, Voice and Verse,
Wed your divine sounds, and mixed power employ,
Dead things with inbreathed sense able to pierce;
And to our high-raised fantasy present
That undisturbed song of pure consent,
Aye sung before the sapphire-colored throne
To him that sits thereon,
With saintly shout and solemn jubilee;
Where the bright Seraphim in burning row
Their loud uplifted angel-trumpets blow,
And the Cherubic host in thousand choirs
Touch their immortal harps of golden wires,
With those just Spirits that wear victorious palms,
Hymns devout and holy psalms
Singing everlastingly:
That we on Earth, with undiscordent voice,
May rightly answer that melodious noise;
As once we did, till disproportioned sin
Jarred against nature's chime, and with harsh din
Broke the fair music that all creatures made
To their great Lord, whose love their motion swayed
In perfect diapason, whilst they stood
In first obedience, and their state of good.
O, may we soon again renew that song,
And keep in tune with Heaven, till God ere long
To his celestial consort us unite,
To live with him, and sing in endless morn of light!

71

On the Morning of Christ's Nativity

This is the Month, and this the happy morn
Wherein the Son of Heaven's eternal King,
Of wedded Maid, and Virgin Mother born,
Our great redemption from above did bring;
For so the holy sages once did sing,
That he our deadly forfeit should release,
And with his Father work us a perpetual peace.

That glorious Form, that Light unsufferable,
And that far-beaming blaze of Majesty,
Wherewith he wont at Heaven's high Council-Table,
To sit amidst the Trinal Unity,
He laid aside; and here with us to be,
Forsook the Courts of everlasting Day,
And chose with us a darksome House of mortal Clay.

Say Heavenly Muse, shall not thy sacred vein
Afford a present to the Infant God?
Hast thou no verse, no hymn, or solemn strain,
To welcome him to this his new abode,
Now while the Heaven by the Sun's team untrod,
Hath took no print of the approaching light,
And all the spangled host keep watch
          in squadrons bright?

See how from far upon the Eastern road
The Star-led Wizards haste with odors sweet:
O run, prevent them with thy humble ode,
And lay it lowly at his blessed feet;
Have thou the honor first, thy Lord to greet,

And join thy voice unto the Angel Choir,
From out his secret Altar touched with hallowed fire.

The Hymn

It was the Winter wild,
While the Heaven-born child,
All meanly wrapped in the rude manger lies;
Nature in awe to him
Had doffed her gaudy trim,
With her great Master so to sympathize:
It was no season then for her
To wanton with the Sun, her lusty Paramour.

Only with speeches fair
She woos the gentle Air
To hide her guilty front with innocent Snow,
And on her naked shame,
Pollute with sinful blame,
The Saintly Veil of Maiden white to throw,
Confounded, that her Maker's eyes
Should look so near upon her foul deformities.

But he her fears to cease,
Sent down the meek-eyed Peace;
She crowned with Olive green, came softly sliding
Down through the turning sphere,
His ready Harbinger,
With Turtle wing the amorous clouds dividing,
And waving wide her myrtle wand,
She strikes a universal Peace through Sea and Land.

No War, or Battle's sound
Was heard the World around:
The idle spear and shield were high up hung;
The hooked Chariot stood
Unstained with hostile blood,
The Trumpet spoke not to the armed throng,
And Kings sat still with awful eye,
As if they surely knew their sovereign Lord was by.

But peaceful was the night
Wherein the Prince of light
His reign of peace upon the earth began:
The Winds, with wonder whist,
Smoothly the waters kissed,
Whispering new joys to the mild Ocean,
Who now hath quite forgot to rave,
While Birds of Calm sit brooding on the charmed wave.

The Stars with deep amaze
Stand fixed in steadfast gaze,
Bending one their precious influence,
And will not take their flight,
For all the morning light,
Or Lucifer that often warned them thence;
But in their glimmering orbs did glow
Until their Lord himself bespoke, and bid them go.

And though the shady gloom
Had given day her room
The Sun himself withheld his wonted speed
And hid his head for shame,
As his inferior flame,
The new-enlightened world no more should need;
He saw a greater Sun appear
Than his bright throne or burning Axeltree could bear.

The Shepherd on the lawn
Or ere the point of dawn
Sat simply chatting in a rustic row;
Full little thought they then
That the mighty Pan
Was kindly come to live with them below;
Perhaps their loves, or else their sheep,
Was all that did their silly thoughts so busy keep.

When such music sweet
Their hearts and ears did greet,
As never was by mortal finger struck,
Divinely-warbled voice
Answering the stringed noise
As all their souls in blissful rapture took:
The Air such pleasure loath to lose,
With thousand echoes still prolongs each heavenly close.

Nature that heard such sound
Beneath the hollow round
Of Cynthia's seat, the Airy region thrilling,
Now was almost won
To think her part was done,
And that her reign had here its last fulfilling;
She knew such harmony alone
Could hold all Heaven and Earth in happier union.

At last surrounds their sight
A Globe of circular light,
That with long beams the shame-faced night arrayed,
The helmeted Cherubim
And sworded Seraphim
Are seen in glittering ranks with wings displayed,
Harping in loud and solemn choir,
With unexpressive notes to Heaven's new-born Heir.

Such Music (as is said)
Before was never made,
But when of old the sons of morning sung,
While the Creator Great
His constellations set,
And the well-balanced world on hinges hung,
And cast the dark foundations deep,
And bid the weltering waves their oozy channel keep.

Ring out you Crystal spheres,
Once bless our human ears,
(If you have power to touch our senses so)
And let your silver chime
Move in melodious time
And let the Bass of Heaven's deep Organ blow,
And with your nine-fold harmony
Make up full consort to the Angelic symphony.

For if such holy Song
Enwrap our fancy long,
Time will run back, and fetch the age of gold,
And speckled vanity
Will sicken soon and die,
And leprous sin will melt from earthly mold,
And Hell itself will pass away,
And leave her dolorous mansions to the peering day.

Yes, Truth and Justice then
Will down return to men,
The enameled Arras of the Rainbow wearing,
And Mercy set between,
Throned in Celestial sheen,
With radiant feet the tissued clouds down steering,
And Heaven as at some festival,
Will open wide the Gates of her high Palace Hall.

But wisest Fate says no,
This must not yet be so,
The Babe lies yet in smiling Infancy,
That on the bitter cross
Must redeem our loss;
So both himself and us to glorify:
Yet first to those enchained in sleep,
The wakeful trump of doom must thunder through the deep,

With such a horrid clang
As on Mount Sinai rang
While the red fire, and smoldering clouds outbrake:
The aged Earth aghast
With terror of that blast,
Shall from the surface to the center shake,
When at the world's last session,
The dreadful Judge in middle air shall spread his throne.

And then at last our bliss
Full and perfect is,
But now begins; for from this happy day
The old Dragon under ground,
In straiter limits bound,
Not half so far casts his usurped sway,
And wroth to see his Kingdom fail,
Swings the scaly horror of his folded tail.

The Oracles are dumb,
No voice or hideous hum
Runs through the arched roof
in words deceiving.
Apollo from his shrine
Can no more divine,
With hollow shriek the steep of Delphos leaving.
No nightly trance, or breathed spell,
Inspires the pale-eyed
Priest from the prophetic cell.

The lonely mountains o'er,
And the resounding shore,
A voice of weeping heard, and loud lament;
From haunted spring and dale
Edged with poplar pale,
The parting Genius is with sighing sent;
With flower-inwoven tresses torn
The Nymphs in twilight shade of tangled thickets mourn.

In consecrated Earth,
And on the holy Hearth,
The Lars and Lemures moan with midnight plaint;
In Urns and Altars round,
A drear and dying sound
Afrights the Flamens at their service quaint;
And the chill Marble seems to sweat,
While each peculiar power forgoes his wonted seat.

Peor and Baalim
Forsake their Temples dim,
With that twice-battered god of Palestine,
And mooned, Ashtaroth,
Heaven's Queen and Mother both,
Now sits not girt with Tapers' holy shine,
The Lybic Hammon shrinks his horn,
In vain the Tyrian Maids their wounded Thammuz mourn.

And sullen Moloch, fled,
Hath left in shadows dread
His burning Idol all of blackest hue;
In vain with Cymbals' ring
They call the grisly king,
In dismal dance about the furnace blue;
The brutish gods of Nile as fast,
Isis and Orus, and the Dog Anubis haste.

Nor is Osiris seen
In Memphian Grove or Green,
Trampling the unshowered Grass with lowings loud:
Nor can he be at rest
Within his sacred chest,
Naught but profoundest Hell can be his shroud:
In vain with Timbreled Anthems dark
The sable-stoled Sorcerers bear his worshipped Ark.

He feels from Judah's Land
The dreaded Infant's hand,
The rays of Bethlehem blind his dusky eyes;
Nor all the gods beside
Longer dare abide,
Nor Typhon huge ending in snaky twine:
Our Babe, to show his Godhead true,
Can in his swaddling bands control the damned crew.

So when the Sun in bed,
Curtained with cloudy red,
Pillows his chin upon an Orient wave,
The locking shadows pale
Troop to the infernal jail;
Each fettered Ghost slips to his several grave,
And the yellow-skirted Fays
Fly after the Night-steeds, leaving their moon-loved maze.

But see! the Virgin blest,
Hath laid her Babe to rest.
Time is our tedious Song should here have ending;
Heaven's youngest-teemed Star
Has fixed her polished Car,
Her sleeping Lord with Handmaid Lamp attending:
And all about the Courtly Stable,
Bright-harnessed Angels sit in order serviceable.

SONNET XIX

On His Blindness

When I consider how my light is spent,
Ere half my days, in this dark world and wide,
And that one Talent which is death to hide,
Lodged with me useless, though my Soul more bent
To serve therewith my Maker, and present
My true account, lest he returning chide;
"Does God exact day-labor, light denied,"
I fondly ask; But patience to prevent
That murmur, soon replies, "God doth not need
Either man's work or his own gifts; who best
Bear his mild yoke, they serve him best; his State
Is Kingly. Thousands at his bidding speed
And post o'er Land and Ocean without rest:
They also serve who only stand and wait."

Thomas Nashe

1567-1601

Thomas Nashe was educated at St. John's College, Cambridge, and became one of the University Wits. He was a master satirist and frequently was the center of controversy. Like other young writers of his time, he was frequently involved in scrapes. He loathed Puritans and was employed by the Church of England to answer attacks made by pamphleteers.

Litany in Time of Plague

Adieu, farewell, earth's bliss;
This world uncertain is;
Fond are life's lustful joys;
Death proves them all but toys;
None from his darts can fly;
I am sick, I must die.
Lord, have mercy on us!

Rich men, trust not in wealth,
Gold cannot buy you health;
Physic himself must fade,
All things to end are made,
The plague full swift goes by;
I am sick, I must die.
Lord, have mercy on us!

Beauty is but a flower
Which wrinkles will devour;
Brightness falls from the air;
Queens have died young and fair;
Dust hath closed Helen's eye.
I am sick, I must die.
Lord have mercy on us!

Strength stoops unto the grave,
Worms feed on Hector brave;

Swords may not fight with fate,
Earth still holds ope her gate.
"Come, come!" the bells do cry.
I am sick, I must die.
Lord, have mercy on us.

Wit with his wantonness
Tasteth death's bitterness;
Hell's executioner
Hath no ears for to hear
What vain art can reply.
I am sick, I must die.
Lord have mercy on us.

Haste, therefore, each degree,
To welcome destiny;
Heaven is our heritage,
Earth but a player's stage;
Mount we unto the sky.
I am sick, I must die.
Lord, have mercy on us.

Sir Walter Ralegh

1552-1618

S ir Walter Ralegh is one of history's more interesting characters. He was imaginative and audacious. Under Queen Elizabeth I, he rose to great prominence, but lost his favor with the queen when he seduced one of her hand-maidens and ended by being executed on a trumped up charge of conspiracy. When King James ascended the throne, Ralegh was tried on a charge of conspiracy and sentenced to death. It was during this period that he wrote The Passionate Man's Pilgrimage. The sentence was later commuted, but Ralegh spent most of the rest of his life imprisoned in the Tower of London. He was released after 16 years and led an expedition to South America, in the course of which, he sacked a Spanish colony. On his return to England, he was arrested and executed on the old charge of conspiracy. Whatever his shortcomings, the poem reveals a man of wit, faith and courage.

The Passionate Mans Pilgrimage,
supposed to be written
by one at the point of death

Give me my Scallop shell of quiet,
My staff of Faith to walk upon,
My Scrip of Joy, Immortal diet,
My bottle of salvation:
My Gown of Glory, hopes true gage,
And thus I'll take my pilgrimage.

Blood must be my bodies balmer,
No other balme will there be given
Whilst my soul like a white Palmer
Travels to the land of heaven,
Over the silver mountains,
Where spring the Nectar fountains:
And there I'll kiss
The Bowl of bliss,
And drink my eternal fill
On every milky hill.
My soul will be a-dry before,
But after, it will never thirst more.

And by the happy blissful way
More peaceful Pilgrims I shall see,
That have shook off their gowns of day,
And go appareled fresh like me.
I'll bring them first
To slake their thirst
And then to taste those Nectar sweetmeats

At the clear wells

Where sweetness dwells,
Drawn up by Saints in Crystal buckets.

And when our bottles and all we,
Are filled with immortality:
Then the holy paths we'll travel
Strewn with Rubies thick as gravel,
Ceilings of Diamonds, Sapphire floors,
High walls of Coral and Pearl Bowers.
From thence to heavens Bribeles hall
Where no corrupted voices brawl,
No Conscience molten into gold,
Nor forged accusers bought and sold,
No cause deferred, nor vain spent Journey,
For there Christ is the king's Attorney:
Who pleads for all without degrees,
And he hath Angels, but no fees.
When the grand twelve million Jury
Of our sins with sinful fury,
Against our souls black verdicts give,
Christ pleads his death, and then we live,
Be thou my speaker taintless pleader,
Unblotted Lawyer, true proceeder,
You move salvation even for alms:
Not with a bribed Lawyers palms.
And this is my eternal plea,
To him that made Heaven, Earth and Sea,
Seeing my flesh must die so soon,
And want a head to dine next noon,
Just at the stroke when my veins start
        and spread
Set on my soul an everlasting head.
Then am I ready like a palmer fit,
To tread those blest paths which before I writ.

Christina Rossetti

1830-1894

Christina Rossetti, the youngest of four children, was overshadowed by her famous brother Dante Gabriel Rossetti. Like many gifted women of her day, she never attended school. She received her education from her mother and from her own reading. However, through her brother she came to know many of the artists of her time. Miss Rossetti had firm religious convictions which led to her rejection of a suitor whose religious views were more liberal than hers. In 1871, she became ill and almost died. For the rest of her life, she was an invalid and rarely left her home, except to attend church services. Her poetry is delicate and often intensely spiritual.

A Better Resurrection

I have no wit, no words, no tears;
My heart within me like a stone
Is numbed too much for hopes or fears.
Look right, look left, I dwell alone;
I lift mine eyes, but dimmed with grief
No everlasting hills I see.
My life is in the falling leaf;
O Jesus, quicken me.

My life is like a faded leaf,
My harvest dwindled to a husk;
Truly my life is void and brief
And tedious in the barren dusk;
My life is like a frozen thing,
No bud nor greenness can I see;
Yet rise it shall—the sap of Spring;
O Jesus rise in me.

My life is like a broken bowl,
A broken bowl that cannot hold
One drop of water for my soul
Or cordial in the searching cold;
Cast in the fire the perished thing;
Melt and remold it, till it be
A royal cup for Him, my King
O Jesus drink of me.

The Heart Knoweth
Its Own Bitterness

Weep yet awhile—
Weep till that day shall dawn when thou shalt smile:
Watch till the day
When all save only love shall pass away.

Weep, sick and lonely,
Bow thy heart to tears.
For none shall guess the secret
of thy griefs and fears.
Weep, till the day dawn,
Refreshing dew:
Weep till the spring:
For genial showers
Bring up the flowers,
And thou shalt sing
In summertime of blossoming.

Heart-sick and silent,
Weep and watch in pain.
Weep for hope perished,
Not to live again:
Weep for love's hope and fear
And passion vain.
Watch till the day
When all save only love shall pass away.

Then love rejoicing
Shall forget to weep;
Shall hope or tear no more,
Or watch, or sleep,
But only love and cease not,
Deep beyond deep.
Now we sow love in tears,
but then shall reap.
Have patience as the Lord's own flock of sheep:
Have patience with His love
Who died below, who lives for thee above.

Advent

This Advent moon shines cold and clear,
These Advent nights are long;
Our lamps have burned year after year,
And still their flame is strong.
"Watchman, what of the night?" we cry,
Heart-sick with hope deferred;
"No speaking signs are in the sky,"
Is still the watchman's word.

The porter watches at the gate,
The servants watch within;
The watch is long betimes and late,
The prize is slow to win.
"Watchman, what of the night?" But still
His answer sounds the same:
"No daybreak tops the utmost hill,
Nor pale our lamps of flame."

One to another hear them speak
The patent virgins wise:
"Surely He is not far to seek"—
"All night we watch and rise."
"The days are evil looking back,
The coming days are dim;
Yet count we not His promise slack,
 But watch and wait for Him."

One with another, soul with soul,
They kindle fire from fire:
"Friends watch us who have touched the goal."

"They urge us come up higher."
"With them shall rest our waysore feet,
With them is built our home,
With Christ." "They sweet, but He most sweet,
Sweeter than honeycomb."

There no more parting, no more pain,
the distant ones brought near,
The lost so long are found again,
Long lost but longer dear;
Eye hath not seen, ear hath not heard,
Nor heart conceived that rest,
With them our good things long deferred,
With Jesus Christ our Best.

We weep because the night is long,
We laugh for day shall rise,
We sing a slow contented song
And knock at Paradise.
Weeping we hold Him fast Who wept
For us, we hold Him fast;
And will not let Him go except
He bless us first or last.

Weeping we hold Him fast tonight;
We will not let Him go
Till daybreak smite our wearied sight
And summer smite the snow.
Then figs shall bud, and dove with dove
Shall coo the livelong day;
Then He shall say, "Arise, My love
My fair one, come away."

John Skelton

1460-1629

John Skelton was a laureate of both Oxford and Cambridge universities. He was well read in four literatures, and was the author of many works and a tutor of the future Henry VIII. Erasmus called him a British literary light. Yet we are not surprised that Alexander Pope, the master of the heroic couplet, called him Beastly Skelton. His poetry has an untamed barbarous air. Indeed, in some ways it prefigures the stream of consciousness of the 20th Century.

Skelton Laureate, Upon A Dead Man's Head That Was Sent To Him From An Honorable Gentlewoman For A Token, Devised This Ghostly Meditation In English, Covenable In Sentence, Commendable, Lamentable, Lacrimable, Profitable For The Soul

Your ugly token
My mind hath broken
From worldly lust,
For I have discussed
We are but dust
And die we must.
It is general
To be mortal:
I have well espied
No man may him hide
From Death hollow-eyed
With sinews withered,
With bones shivered,
With his worm-eaten maw,
And his ghastly jaw
Gasping aside,
Naked of hide,
Neither flesh nor fell.
Then by my counsel
Look that ye spell
Well this gospel,
For where so we dwell
Death will us quell
And with us mell.
For all our pampered paunches
There may no fraunchis

Nor worldly bliss
Redeem us from this:
Our days be dated
To be checkmated
With drawttis of Death,
Stopping our breath;
Our eyes sinking,
Our bodies stinking,
Our gums grinning,
Our souls brinning.
To whom, then, shall we sue
For to have rescue
But to sweet Jesus
On us then for to rue?
O goodly Child
Of Mary mild,
Then be our shield,
That we be not exiled
To the dyne dale
Of bottomless bale,
Nor to the lake
Of fiends black.
But grant us grace
To see Thy face,
And to purchase
Thine heavenly place,
And thy palace
Full of solace
Above the sky
That is so high,
Eternally
To behold and see
The Trinity.
  Amen.

Mirres vovs y.

Robert Southwell

1561-1595

Robert Southwell was a Jesuit and a martyr. He studied at the English College in Rome and underwent a gruesome martyrdom at Tyburn. His English poetry was not published until after his death, when it enjoyed wide popularity.

The Burning Babe

As I in hoary winter's night stood shivering in the snow,
Surprised I was with sudden heat which made my heart
to   glow;
And lifting up a fearful eye to view what fire was near,
A pretty babe all burning bright did in the air appear;
Who, scorched with excessive heat, such floods of tears
    did shed
As though his floods should quench his flames, which
    with his tears were fed.
"Alas," quoth he, "but newly born in fiery heats I fry,
Yet none approach to warm their hearts or feel my fire but I;
My faultless breast the furnace is, the fuel wounding thorns;
Love is the fire and sighs the smoke, the ashes shames
    and scorns;
The fuel Justice layeth on, and Mercy blows the coals;
The metal in this furnace wrought are men's defiled souls,
For which as now on fire I am to work them to their good,
So will I melt into a bath to wash them in my blood."
With this he vanish'd out of sight and swiftly shrunk away,
And straight I called unto mind that it was Christmas day.

Seek Flowers of Heaven

Soar up, my soul, unto thy rest,
cast off this loathsome load;
Long is the date of thy exile,
too long the strict abode;
Graze not on worldly withered weed,
it fitteth not thy taste;
The flowers of everlasting spring
do grow for thy repaste.
Their leaves are stained in beauty's dye
and blazed with their beams,
Their stalks enameled with delight
and limmed with glorious gleams;
Life-giving juice of living love
their sugared veins doth fill,
And watered with everlasting showers
they nectared drops distill.
These flowers do spring from fertile soil,
though from unmanured field;
Most glittering gold in lieu of glebe
these fragrant flowers do yield,
Whose sovereign scent, surpassing sense,
so ravisheth the mind
That worldly weeds needs must he loath
that can these flowers find.

Edmund Spenser

1552-1599

Edmund Spenser has never been a 'popular' poet in the sense that Shakespeare, Milton, Keats and other great English poets are popular. His poetry is too rarefied ever to achieve the wide appeal that other major poets have. Nevertheless, Spenser is a master, and those who spend time with him will be amply rewarded. Spenser spent a portion of his career as secretary to Lord Grey de Wilton, the Lord Deputy of Ireland, and Spenser benefited from Lord Grey's heavy handed. In the end, his involvement in Ireland probably kept him for completing his great masterpiece, The Faerie Queen.

In 1598, he fled an Irish uprising in order to save his life. He died the next year, perhaps from a sickness brought on by his experience. He was buried in Westminster Abbey. Two centuries later, Charles Lamb called him, "The poet's poet."

Sonnet XVIII

Most glorious Lord of life, that on this day,
did make thy triumph over death and sin:
and having harrowed hell, did bring away
captivity thence captive us to win:

This joyous day, dear Lord, with joy begin,
and grant that we for whom thou died
being with thy dear blood clean washed from sin,
may live for ever in felicity.

And that thy love we weighing worthily,
may likewise love thee for the same again:
and for thy sake that all like dear did buy, with
love may one another entertain.

So let us love, dear love, Like as we ought,
love is the lesson which the Lord us taught.

A Hymn of Heavenly Love

Love, lift me up upon thy golden wings,
From this base world unto thy heavens height,
Where I may see those admirable things,
Which there thou work by thy sovereign might,
are above feeble reach of earthly sight,
That I thereof an heavenly Hymn may sing
Unto the god of Love, high heavens king.

Many lewd layes (ah woe is me the more)
In praise of that mad fit, which fools call love,
I have in the heat of youth made heretofore,
That in light wits did loose affection move.
But all those follies now I do reprove,
And turned have the tenor of my string,
The heavenly praises of true love to sing.
And ye that wont with greedy vain desire
read my fault, and wondering at my fame,
warm your selves at my wide sparkling fire,
Since now that heat is quenched, quench my blame,
And in her ashes shroud my dying shame:
For who my passed follies now pursues,
Begins his own, and my old fault renews.
Before this worlds great frame, in which all things
Are now contained, found any being place,
Ere flitting Time could wag his eyas wings
About that mighty bound, which doth embrace
The rolling Spheres, and parts their hours by space,
That high eternal power, which now doth move
In all these things, moved in it self by love.

It loved it self, because it self was faire;
(For faire is loved;) and of it self begot

Like to it self his eldest son and heir,
Eternal, pure, and void of sinful blot,
The firstling of his joy, in whom no jot
Of loves dislike, or pride was to be found,
Whom he therefore with equal honor crowned.

With him he reigned, before all time prescribed,
In endless glory and immortal might,
Together with that third from them derived,
Most wise, most holy, most almighty Spright,
Whose kingdoms throne no thought of earthly wight
Can comprehend, much less my trembling verse
With equal words can hope it to rehearse.

Yet O most blessed Spirit, pure lamp of light,
Eternal spring of grace and wisdom true,
Vouchsafe to shed into my barren spright,
Some little drop of thy celestial dew,
That may my rhymes with sweet infuse embrew,
And give me words equal to my thought,
To tell the marvels by thy mercy wrought.

Yet being pregnant still with powerful grace,
And full of fruitful love, that loves to get
Things like himself, and to enlarge his race,
His second brood though not in power so great,
An infinite increase of Angels bright,
All glistening glorious in their Makers light.

To them the heavens illimitable height,
Not this round heaven, which we from hence behold,
Adorned with thousand lamps of burning light,
And with ten thousand gems of shining gold,
He gave as their inheritance to hold,

That they might serve him in eternal bliss,
And be partakers of those joys of his.

There they in their trinal triplicities
About him wait, and on his will depend,
Either with nimble wings to cut the skies,
When he them on his messages doth send,
Or on his own dread presence to attend,
Where they behold the glory of his light,
And carol Hymns of love both day and night.

Both day and night is to them all one,
For he his beams doth still to them extend,
That darkness there appears never none,
Ne hath their day, ne hath their bliss an end,
But there their termless time in pleasure spend,
Ne ever should their happiness decay,
Had not they dared their Lord to disobey.

But pride impatient of long resting peace,
Did puff them up with greedy bold ambition,
That they began to cast their state how to increase,
Above the fortune of their first condition,
And sit in God's own seat without commission:
The brightest Angel, even the Child of light
Drew millions more against their God to fight.

The Almighty seeing their so bold assay,
Kindled the flame of his consuming fire,
And with his only breath them blew away
From heaven's height, to which they did aspire,
To deepest hell, and lake of damned fire;
Where they in darkness and dread horror dwell.
Hating the happy light from which they fell.

So that next off-spring of the Maker's love,
Next to himself in glorious degree,
Degendering to hate, fell from above
Through pride; (for pride and love may ill agree)
And now of sin to all example be:
How then can sinful flesh itself assure,
Since purest Angels fell to be impure.

But that eternal fount of love and grace,
Still flowing forth his goodness to all,
Now seeing left a waste and empty place
In his wide Palace, through those Angels fall,
Cast to supply the same, and to install
A new unknown Colony therein,
Whose root from earth's base groundwork should begin.

Therefore of clay, base,vile, and next to nought,
Yet formed by wondrous skill, and by his might:
According to an heavenly pattern wrought,
Which he had fashioned in his wise foresight,
He man did make, and breathed a living spright
Into his face most beautiful and fair,
Endowed with wisdom riches, heavenly, rare.

Such he him made, that he resemble might
Himself, as mortal thing immortal could;
Him to be Lord of every living wight,
He made by love out of his own like mould,
In whom he might his mighty self behold:
For love doth love the thing beloved to see,
That like itself in lovely shape may be.

But man forgetful of his makers grace,
No less then Angels, whom he did ensew,

Fell from the hope of promised heavenly place,
Into the mouth of death, to sinners dew,
And all his off-spring into thraldom threw:
Where they forever should in bonds remain,
Of never dead, yet ever dying paine.

Till that great Lord of Love, which him at first
Made of mere love, and after liked well,
Seeing him lie like creature long accurst,
In that deep horror of despaired hell,
Him wretch in doole would let no longer dwell,
But cast out of that bondage to redeem,
And pay the price, all were his debt extreme.

Out of the bosom of eternal bliss,
In which he reigned with his glorious sire,
He down descended, like a most demisse
And abject thrall, in flesh's frail attire,
That he for him might pay sin deadly hire,
And him restore to that happy state,
In which he stood before his hapless fate.

In flesh at first the guilt committed was,
Therefore in flesh it must be satisfied:
Nor spirit, nor Angel, though they man surpass,
Could make amends to God for mans misguide,
But only man himself, who self did slide.
So taking flesh of sacred virgins womb,
For man's dear sake he did a man become.

And that most blessed body, which was borne
Without all blemish or reproachful blame,
He freely gave to be both rent and torn
Of cruel hands, who with despightful shame

Reviling him, that them most vile became,
At length him nailed on a gallows tree,
And slew the just, by most unjust decree.

O hue and most unspeakable impression
Of loves deep wound, that pierced the piteous hart
Of that dear Lord with so entire affection,
And sharply launching every inner part,
Dolors of death into his soul did dart;
Doing him die, that never it deserved,
To free his foes, that from his heast had swerved.

What heart can feel least touch of so sore launch,
Or thought can think the depth of so dear wound?
Whose bleeding source their streams yet never staunch,
But still do flow, and freshly still redound,
To heal the sores of sinful souls unsound,
And cleanse the guilt of that infected crime,
Which was enrooted in all fleshly slime.

O blessed well of love, O flower of grace,
O glorious Morning-star, O lamp of light,
Most lively image of thy fathers face,
Eternal King of glory, Lord of might,
Meek lamb of God before all worlds behight,
How can we thee requite for all this good?
Or what can prize that thy most precious blood?

Yet nought thou asked in lieu of all this love;
But love of us for guerdon of thy paine.
Aye me; what can us less then that behove?
Had he required life of us again,
Had it been wrong to ask his own with gain?
He gave us life, he it restored lost;

Then life were least, that us so little cost.

But he Our life hath left unto us free,
Free that was thrall, and blessed that was band;
Nor ought demands, but that we loving bee,
As he himself hath loved us beforehand,
And bound thereto with an eternal band,
Him first to love, that us so dearly bought,
And next, our brethren to his image wrought.

Him first to love, great right and reason is,
Who first to us our life and being gave;
And after when we fared had amiss,
Us wretches from the second death did save;
And last the food of life, which now we have,
Even himself in his dear sacrament,
To feed our hungry souls to us lent.

Then next to love our brethren, that were made
Of that self mould, and that self makers hand,
That we, and to the same again shall fade,
Where they shall have like heritage of land,
How ever here on higher steps we stand;
Which also were with self same price redeemed
That we, how ever of us light esteemed.

And were they not, yet since that loving Lord
Commanded us to love them for his sake,
Even for his sake, and for his sacred word,
Which in his last bequest he to us spake,
We should them love, and with their needs partake;
Knowing that whatsoever to them we give,
We give to him, by whom we all doe live.
Such mercy he by his most holy reed

To us taught, and to approve it true,
Exampled it by his most righteous deed,
Showing us mercy miserable crew,
That we the like should to the wretches shew,
And love our brethren; thereby to approve,
How much himself that loved us, we love.

Then rouse thy self, O earth, out of thy soil,
In which thou wallows like to filthy swine,
And doest thy mind in dirty pleasures moyle,
Unmindful of that dearest Lord of thine;
Lift up to him thy heavy clouded eyes,
That thou his sovereign bounty may behold,
And read through love his mercies manifold.

Begin from first, where he encradled was
In simple cratch, wrapped in a wad of hay,
Between the toilful Ox and humble Ass,
And in what rags, and in how base array,
The glory of our heavenly riches lay,
When him the silly Shepherds came to see,
Whom greatest Princes sought on lowest knee.

From thence read on the story of his life,
His humble carriage, his unfaulty way,
His cankered foes, his fights, his toil, his strife,
His pains, his poverty, his sharp assays,
Through which he past his miserable days,
Offending none, and doing good to all,
Yet being maligned both of great and small.

And look at last how of most wretched wights,
He taken was, betrayed, and false accused,
How with most scornful taunts, and fell despises

He was reviled, disgraced, and foully abused.
How scourged, how crowned, how buffeted,
   how bruised;
And lastly how twixt robbers crucified,
With bitter wounds through hands, through feet and side,

Then let thy flinty heart that feels no paine,
Empierced be with pitiful remorse,
And let thy bowels bleed in every vein,
At sight of his most sacred heavenly corpse,
So torn and mangled with malicious force,
And let thy soul, whose sins his sorrows wrought,
Melt into tears, and groan in grieved thought.

With sense whereof whilst so thy softened spirit
Is only touched, and humbled with meek zeal,
Through meditation of his endless merit,
Lift up thy mind to the author of thy weal,
And to his sovereign mercy doe appeal;
Learn him to love, that loved thee so dear,
And in thy breast his blessed image bear.

With all thy heart, with all thy soul and mind,
Thou must him love, and his behests embrace:
All other loves, with which the world doth blind
Weak fancies, and stir up affections base,
Thou must renounce, and utterly displace,
And give thy self to him full and free,
That full and freely gave himself to thee.

Then shalt thou feel thy spirit so possessed,
And ravished with devouring great desire
Of his dear self, that shall thy feeble breast
Inflame with love, and set thee all on fire

With burning zeal, through every part entire,
That in no earthly thing thou shalt delight,
But in his sweet and amiable sight.

Thenceforth all worlds desire will in thee dye,
And all earths glory on which men do gaze,
Seemed dirt and dross in thy pure sighted eye,
Compared to that celestial beauties blaze,
Whose glorious beams all fleshly sense doth daze
With admiration of their passing light,
Blinding the eyes and illumining the spright.

Then shall thy ravished soul inspired be
With heavenly thoughts, far above human skill,
And thy bright radiant eyes shall plainly see
The Idea of his pure glory, present still,
Before thy face, that all thy spirits shall fill
With sweet enragement of celestial love,
Kindled through sight of those faire things above.

Francis Thompson

1859-1907

Francis Thompson was a drug addict who lived on the streets of London from 1885 to 1888. Originally he had planned to become a Catholic priest but failed to qualify. Next he planned a career in medicine but failed at that too. He was rescued from the streets and from death by Wilfred and Alice Meynell. He recovered from his drug addiction at a priory and later at a monastery. The Hound of Heaven is one of the great poems dealing with religious experience. Thompson died of tuberculosis in London in 1907.

The Hound of Heaven

I fled Him, down the nights and down the days;
   I fled Him, down the arches of the years;
I fled Him, down the labyrinthine ways
   Of my own mind; and in the midst of tears
I hid from Him, and under running laughter.
      Up vistaed slopes I sped;
      And shot, precipitated,
Adown Titanic glooms of chasmed fears
   From those strong Feet that followed, followed after.
      But with unhurrying chase,
      And unperturbed pace,
     Deliberate speed, majestic instancy,
      They beat—and a Voice beat
      More instant than the Feet
     "All things betray thee, who betrayest Me "

      I pleaded, outlaw-wise,
By many a hearted casement, curtained red,
   Trellised with intertwining charities
(For, though I knew his love Who followed,
      Yet was I sore adread
Lest, having Him, I must have naught beside);
But, if one little casement parted wide,
   The gust of his approach would clash it to.
   Fear wist not to evade, as Love wist to pursue.
Across the margent of the world I fled,
   And troubled the gold gateways of the stars,
   Smiting for shelter on the clanged bars;
     Fretted to dulcet jars
And silvern chatter the pale ports o' the moon.
I said to dawn, Be sudden; to eve, Be soon;

121

With they young skyey blossoms heap me over
From this tremendous Lover!
Float thy vague veil about me, lest He see!
I tempted all His servitors, but to find
My own betrayal in their constancy,
In faith to Him their fickleness to me,
Their traitorous trueness, and their loyal deceit.
To all swift things for swiftness did I sue;
Clung to the whistling mane of every wind.
But whether they swept, smoothly fleet,
The long savannahs of the blue;
Or whether, Thunder-driven,
They clanged his chariot 'thwart a heaven
Plashy with flying lightning round the spurn o' their feet—
Fear wist not to evade as Love wist to pursue.
Still with unhurrying chase,
And unperturbed pace,
Deliberate speed, majestic instancy,
Came on the following Feet,
And a Voice above their beat—
"Naught shelters thee, who wilt not shelter Me."

I sought no more that after which I strayed
In face of man or maid;
But still within the little children's eyes
Seems something, something that replies;
They at least are for me, surely for me!
I turned me to them very wistfully
But, just as their young eyes grew sudden fair
With dawning answers there,
Their angel plucked them from me by the hair
"Come then, ye other children, Nature's—share
With me" (said I) "your delicate fellowship;
Let me greet you lip to lip,

Let me twine with you caresses
    Wantoning
With our Lady-Mother's vagrant tresses,
    Banqueting
With her in her wind-walled palace,
Underneath her azured dais,
Quaffing, as your taintless way is,
    From a chalice
Lucent-weeping out of the dayspring."
    So it was done
I in their delicate fellowship was one—
Drew the bolt of Nature's secrecies.
    I knew all the swift importings
    On the willful face of skies;
    I knew how the clouds arise
    Spumed of the wild sea-snortings;
    All that's born or dies
    Rose and drooped with—made them shapers
Of mine own moods, or wailful or divine—
    With them joyed and was bereaven.
    I was heavy with the even,
    When she lit her glimmering tapers
    Round the day's dead sanctities.
    I laughed in the morning's eyes.
I triumphed and I saddened with all weather,
    Heaven and I wept together,
And its sweet tears were salt with mortal mine;
Against the red throb of its sunset-heart
    I laid my own to beat,
    And share commingling heat;
But not by that, by that, was eased my human smart.
In vain my tears were wet on Heaven's gray cheek.
For ah! we know not what each other says,
    These things and I, in sound I speak—

123

Their sound is but their stir, they speak by silences.
Nature, poor stepdame, cannot slake my drouth;
          Let her, if she would owe me,
Drop yon blue bosom-veil of sky, and show me
          The breasts o'her tenderness;
Never did any milk of hers once bless
          My thirsting mouth.
          Nigh and nigh draws the chase,
          With unperturbed pace,
          Deliberate speed, majestic instancy;
          And past those noised Feet
          A voice comes yet more fleet—
"Lo naught contents thee, who content'st not Me."

Naked I wait Thy love's uplifted stroke!
My harness piece by piece Thou hast hewn from me,
          And smitten me to my knee;
      I am defenseless utterly.
      I slept, methinks, and woke,
And, slowly gazing, find me stripped in sleep.
In the rash lustihead of my young powers
      I shook the pillaring hours
And pulled my life upon me; grimed with smears,
I stand amid the dust o' the mounded years—
My mangled youth lies dead beneath the heap.
My days have crackled and gone up in smoke,
Have puffed and burst as sun-starts on a stream.
      Yea, faileth now even dream
The dreamer, and the lute the lutanist;
Even the linked fantasies, in whose blossomy twist
I swung the earth a trinket at my wrist,
Are yielding; cords of all too weak account
For earth with heavy griefs so overplussed.
      Ah! is Thy love indeed

A weed, albeit an amaranthine weed,
Suffering no flowers except its own to mount?
           Ah! must—
           Designer infinite!—
Ah! must Thou char the wood ere Thou canst limn with it?
My freshness spent its wavering shower I' the dust;
And now my heart is as a broken fount,
Wherein tear-drippings stagnate, spilt down ever
               From the dank thoughts that shiver
Upon the sightful branches of my mind.
           Such is; what is to be?
The pulp so bitter, how shall taste the rind?
I dimly guess what Time in mists confounds;
Yet ever and anon a trumpet sounds
From the hid battlements of Eternity;
Those shaken mists a space unsettle, then
Round the half-glimpsed turrets slowly wash again.
           But not ere him who summoneth
           I first have seen, enwound
With glooming robes purpureal, cypress-crowned;
His name I know, and what his trumpet saith.
Whether man's heart or life it be which yields
           Thee harvest, must Thy harvest fields
           Be dunged with rotten death?

           Now of that long pursuit
           Comes on at hand the bruit;
           That Voice is round me like a bursting sea:
           "And is thy earth so marred,
           Shattered in shard on shard?
           Lo, all things fly thee, for thou fliest Me!
           Strange, piteous, futile thing,
Wherefore should any set thee love apart?
Seeing none, but I makes much of naught" (He said)

"And human love needs human meriting,
How hast thou merited—
Of all man's clotted clay the dingiest clot?
Alack, thou knowest not
How little worthy of any love thou art!
Whom wilt thou find to love ignoble thee
Save Me, save only Me?
All which I took from thee I did but take,
Not for thy harms
But just that thou might'st seek it in My arms.
All which thy child's mistake
Fancies as lost, I have stored for thee at home;
Rise, clasp My hand, and come!"

Halts by me that footfall;
Is my gloom, after all,
Shade of His hand, outstretched caressingly?
"Ah, fondest, blindest, weakest,
I am He Whom thou seekest!
Thou dravest love from thee, who dravest Me."

The Kingdom of God

'In no Strange Land'

O world invisible we view thee
O world intangible, we touch thee,
O world unknowable, we know thee,
Inapprehensible, we clutch thee!

Does the fish soar to find the ocean,
The eagle plunge to find the air—
That we ask of the stars in motion,
If they have rumor of thee there?

Not where the wheeling systems darken,
And our benumbed conceiving soars! —
The drift of pinions would we hearken,
Beats at our own clay-shuttered doors.

The angels keep their ancient places—
Turn but a stone and start a wing!
'Tis ye, 'tis your estranged faces,
That miss the many-splendored thing.

But (when so sad thou canst not sadder)
Cry—and upon thy so sore loss
Shall shine the traffic of Jacob's ladder
Pitched betwixt Heaven and Charing Cross.

Yea, in the night, my Soul, my daughter,
Cry—clinging Heaven by the hems;
And lo, Christ walking on the water,
Not of Genesareth, but Thames!

Thomas Traherne

1636-1674

Thomas Traherne was a writer of religious poetry and prose tracts. His most important prose works were published after his death. Christian Ethicks was published in 1675 and Centuries of Meditations was published in 1909. A number of his manuscripts were discover in 1896 and were published for the first time in 1903.

Wonder

How like an angel came I down
    How bright are all things here!
When first among His works I did appear,
    O how their glory me did crown!
The world resembled His eternity,
    In which my soul did walk;
And everything that I did see
    Did with me talk.

The skies in their magnificence,
    The lively, lovely air,
Oh, how divine, how soft, how sweet, how fair!
    The stars did entertain my sense;
And all the works of God so bright and pure,
    So rich and great did seem
As if they ever must endure
    In my esteem.

A native health and innocence
    Within my bones did grow;
And while my God did all his glories show,
    I felt a vigor in my sense
That was all spirit: I within did flow
    With seas of life like wine;
I nothing in the world did know
    But 'twas divine.

Harsh, ragged objects were concealed:
    Oppressions, tears, and cries,

Sins, griefs, complaints, dissentions, weeping eyes
    Were hid, and only things revealed
Which heavenly spirits and the angels prize.
    The state of innocence
And bliss, not trades and poverties,
    Did fill my sense.

The streets were paved with golden stones;
    The boys and girls were mine:
Oh, how did all their lovely faces shine!
    The sons of men were holy ones;
In joy and beauty they appeared to me;
    And everything which here I found,
While like an angel I did see,
    Adorned the ground.

Rich diamond and pearl and gold
    In every place was seen;
Rare splendors, yellow, blue, red, white, and green,
    Mine eyes did everywhere behold.
Great wonders clothed with glory did appear;
    Amazement was my bliss;
That and my wealth was everywhere;
    No joy to this!

Cursed and devised proprieties,
    With envy, avarice,
And fraud, those fiends that spoil even Paradise,
    Flew from the splendor of mine eyes;
And so did hedges, ditches, limits, bounds:
    I dreamed not aught of those,
But wandered over all men's grounds,
    And found repose.

Proprieties themselves were mine,
    And hedges ornaments;
Walls, boxes, coffers, and their rich contents
    Did not divide my joys but all combine.
Clothes, ribbons, jewels, laces I esteemed
    My Joys by others worn;
For me they all to wear them seemed
    When I was born.

Henry Vaughan

1622-1695

Henry Vaughan was a native of Wales who studied at Oxford, studied law in London, probably served as a soldier, and ended his years a a country doctor in Wales.

The World

I saw Eternity the other night,
Like a great ring of pure and endless light,
All calm, as it was bright;
And round beneath it, Time, in hours, days, years
Driven by the spheres
Like a vast shadow moved; in which the world
And all her train were hurled.

The doting lover in his quaintest strain
Did there complain;
Near him, his lute, his fancy, and his flights,
Wit's sour delights
With gloves, and knots, the silly snares of pleasure,
Yet his dear treasure,
All scattered lay, while he his eyes did pour
Upon a flower.

The darksome statesman, hung with weights and woe,
Like a thick midnight-fog moved there so slow
He did not stay, nor go;
Condemning thoughts, like sad eclipses, scowl
Upon his soul,
And clouds of crying witnesses without
Pursued him with one shout.
Yet digged the mole, and lest his ways be found,
Worked under ground,
Where he did clutch his prey; but one did see
That policy;
Churches and altars fed him; perjuries
Were gnats and flies;
It rained about him blood and tears, but he

Drank them as free.

The fearful miser on a heap of rust
Sat pining all his life there, did scarce trust
His own hands with the dust,
Yet would not place one piece above, but lives
In fear of thieves.
Thousands there were as frantic as himself,
And hugged each one his pelf;
The downright epicure placed heaven in sense,
And scorned pretense;
While others, slipped into a wide excess,
Said little less;
The weaker sort, slight, trivial wares enslave,
Who think them brave;
And poor, despised Truth sat counting by
Their victory.

Yet some, who all this while did weep and sing,
And sing and weep, soared up into the ring;
But most would use no wing.
O fools, said I, thus to prefer dark night
Before true light!
To live in grots and caves, and hate the day
Because it shows the way,
The way, which from this dead and dark abode
Leads up to God;
A way where you might tread the sun, and be
More bright than he!
But, as I did their madness so discuss,
One whispered thus
This ring the Bridegroom did for none provide,
But for his bride.

The Retreat

Happy those early days, when I
Shined in my angel-infancy!
Before I understood this place
Appointed for my second race,
Or taught my soul to fancy aught
But a white, celestial thought;
when yet I had not walked above
A mile or two from my first love,
And looking back at that short space,
Could see a glimpse of his bright face;
When on some gilded cloud or flower
My gazing soul would dwell an hour,
And in those weaker glories spy
Some shadows of eternity;
Before I taught my tongue to wound
My conscience with a sinful sound,
Or had the black art to dispense,
A several sin to every sense,
But felt through all this fleshly dress
Bright shoots of everlastingness.
Oh, how I long to travel back,
And tread again that ancient track,
That I might once more reach that plain,
Where first I left my glorious train;
From whence the enlightened spirit sees
that shady city of palm trees.
But ah! My soul with too much stay
Is drunk, and staggers in the way!
Some men a forward motion love,
But I by backward steps would move;
And when this dust falls to the urn,
In that state I came, return.

Oscar Wilde

1854-1905

Oscar Wilde was a man who was plagued by morality. He was brilliant, witty, and sarcastic, and an aesthete. He left his wife and children for the homosexual lifestyle, and became a kind of flash-point in Victorian society even, for example, being a subject of satire for Gilbert and Sullivan. Wilde's downfall came after he brought a libel suit against the Marquess of Queensbury, whose son he was involved with. The suit was dismissed, but it led to charges of sexual immorality against Wilde. He was convicted and sentenced to two years in prison. Two great works, De Profundis, and The Ballad of Reading Gaol, were written after he was released for prison. He spent the rest of his life as an exile in Paris. The liberty of substituting the word 'jail' for 'gaol' has been taken to make the ballad more accessible to American readers.

The Ballad of Reading Jail

In memoriam C.T.W.
sometime trooper of the Royal Horse Guards
obiit H.M. prison, Reading, Berkshire, July 7, 1896

I

He did not wear his scarlet coat,
   For blood and wine are red,
And blood and wine were on his hands
   When they found him with the dead,
The poor dead woman whom he loved,
   And murdered in her bed.

He walked amongst the Trial Men
   In a suit of shabby grey;
A cricket cap was on his head,
   And his step seemed light and gay;
But I never saw a man who looked
   So wistfully at the day.

I never saw a man who looked
   With such a wistful eye
Upon that little tent of blue
   Which prisoners call the sky,
And at every drifting cloud that went
   With sails of silver by.

I walked, with other souls in pain,
   Within another ring,
And was wondering if the man had done
   A great or little thing,
When a voice behind me whispered low,
   "That fellow's got to swing."

143

Dear Christ! the very prison walls
    Suddenly seemed to reel,
And the sky above my head became
    Like a casque of scorching steel;
And, though I was a soul in pain,
    My pain I could not feel.

I only knew what hunted thought
    Quickened his step, and why
He looked upon the garish day
    With such a wistful eye;
The man had killed the thing he loved,
    And so he had to die.

Yet each man kills the thing he loves,
    By each let this be heard,
Some do it with a bitter look,
    Some with a flattering word,
The coward does it with a kiss,
    The brave man with a sword!

Some kill their love when they are young,
    And some when they are old;
Some strangle with the hands of Lust,
    Some with the hands of Gold:
The kindest use a knife, because
    The dead so soon grow cold.

Some love too little, some too long,
    Some sell, and others buy;
Some do the deed with many tears,
    And some without a sigh:
For each man kills the thing he loves,
    Yet each man does not die.

He does not die a death of shame

On a day of dark disgrace,
Nor have a noose about his neck,
  Nor a cloth upon his face,
Nor drop feet foremost through the floor
  Into an empty space.

He does not sit with silent men
  Who watch him night and day;
Who watch him when he tries to weep,
  And when he tries to pray;
Who watch him lest himself should rob
  The prison of its prey.

He does not wake at dawn to see
  Dread figures throng his room,
The shivering Chaplain robed in white,
  The Sheriff stern with gloom,
And the Governor all in shiny black,
  With the yellow face of Doom.

He does not rise in piteous haste
  To put on convict-clothes,
While some coarse-mouthed Doctor gloats, and notes
  Each new and nerve-twitched pose,
Fingering a watch whose little ticks
  Are like horrible hammer-blows.

He does not feel that sickening thirst
  That sands one's throat, before
The hangman with his gardener's gloves
  Comes through the padded door,
And binds one with three leathern thongs,
  That the throat may thirst no more.

He does not bend his head to hear
  The Burial Office read,

Nor, while the anguish of his soul
    Tells him he is not dead,
Cross his own coffin, as he moves
    Into the hideous shed.

He does not stare upon the air
    Through a little roof of glass:
He does not pray with lips of clay
    For his agony to pass;
Nor feel upon his shuddering cheek
    The kiss of Caiaphas.

II

Six weeks the guardsman walked the yard
    In the suit of shabby grey:
His cricket cap was on his head,
    And his step seemed light and gay,
But I never saw a man who looked
    So wistfully at the day.

I never saw a man who looked
    With such a wistful eye
Upon that little tent of blue
    Which prisoners call the sky,
And at every wandering cloud that trailed
    Its ravelled fleeces by.

He did not wring his hands, as do
    Those witless men who dare
To try to rear the changeling Hope
    In the cave of black Despair:
He only looked upon the sun,
    And drank the morning air.

He did not wring his hands nor weep,

Nor did he peek or pine,
But he drank the air as though it held
    Some healthful anodyne;
With open mouth he drank the sun
    As though it had been wine

And I and all the souls in pain,
    Who tramped the other ring,
Forgot if we ourselves had done
    A great or little thing,
And watched with gaze of dull amaze
    The man who had to swing.

For strange it was to see him pass
    With a step so light and gay,
And strange it was to see him look
    So wistfully at the day,
And strange it was to think that he
    Had such a debt to pay.

For oak and elm have pleasant leaves
    That in the spring-time shoot:
But grim to see is the gallows-tree,
    With its adder-bitten root,
And, green or dry, a man must die
    Before it bears its fruit!

The loftiest place is that seat of grace
    For which all worldlings try:
But who would stand in hempen band
    Upon a scaffold high,
And through a murderer's collar take
    His last look at the sky?

It is sweet to dance to violins
    When Love and Life are fair:

To dance to flutes, to dance to lutes
    Is delicate and rare:
But it is not sweet with nimble feet
    To dance upon the air!

So with curious eye and sick surmise
    We watched him day by day,
And wondered if each one of us
    Would end the self-same way,
For none can tell to what red Hell
    His sightless soul may stray.

At last the dead man walked no more
    Amongst the Trial Men,
And I knew that he was standing up
    In the black dock's dreadful pen,
And that never would I see his face
    For weal or woe again.

Like two doomed ships that pass in storm
    We had crossed each other's way:
But we made no sign, we said no word,
    We had no word to say;
For we did not meet in the holy night,
    But in the shameful day.

A prison wall was round us both,
    Two outcast men we were:
The world had thrust us from its heart,
    And God from out His care:
And the iron gin that waits for Sin
    Had caught us in its snare.

III

In Debtors' Yard the stones are hard,
    And the dripping wall is high,

So it was there he took his air
    Beneath the leaden sky,
And by each side a warder walked,
    For fear the man might die.

Or else he sat with those who watched
    His anguish night and day;
Who watched him when he rose to weep,
    And when he crouched to pray;
Who watched him lest himself should rob
    Their scaffold of its prey.

The Governor was strong upon
    The Regulations Act:
The Doctor said that Death was but
    A scientific fact:
And twice a day the Chaplain called,
    And left a little tract.

And twice a day he smoked his pipe,
    And drank his quart of beer:
His soul was resolute, and held
    No hiding-place for fear;
He often said that he was glad
    The hangman's day was near.

But why he said so strange a thing
    No warder dared to ask:
For he to whom a watcher's doom
    Is given as his task,
Must set a lock upon his lips
    And make his face a mask.

Or else he might be moved, and try
    To comfort or console:
And what should Human Pity do

Pent up in Murderer's Hole?
What word of grace in such a place
    Could help a brother's soul?

With slouch and swing around the ring
    We trod the Fools' Parade!
We did not care: we knew we were
    The Devil's Own Brigade:
And shaven head and feet of lead
    Make a merry masquerade.

We tore the tarry rope to shreds
    With blunt and bleeding nails;
We rubbed the doors, and scrubbed the floors,
    And cleaned the shining rails:
And, rank by rank, we soaped the plank
    And clattered with the pails.

We sewed the sacks, we broke the stones
    We turned the dusty drill:
We banged the tins, and bawled the hymns,
    And sweated on the mill:
But in the heart of every man
    Terror was lying still.

So still it lay that every day
    Crawled like a weed-clogged wave:
And we forgot the bitter lot
    That waits for fool and knave,
Till once, as we tramped in from work,
    We passed an open grave.

With yawning mouth the yellow hole
    Gaped for a living thing;
The very mud cried out for blood
    To the thirsty asphalt ring;

And we knew that ere one dawn grew fair
    Some prisoner had to swing.

Right in we went, with soul intent
    On Death and Dread and Doom:
The hangman, with his little bag,
    Went shuffling through the gloom:
And I trembled as I groped my way
    Into my numbered tomb.

That night the empty corridors
    Were full of forms of Fear,
And up and down the iron town
    Stole feet we could not hear
And through the bars that hide the stars
    White faces seemed to peer.

He lay as one who lies and dreams
    In a pleasant meadow-land,
The watchers watched him as he slept,
    And could not understand
How one could sleep so sweet a sleep
    With a hangman close at hand.

But there is no sleep when men must weep
    Who never yet have wept:
So we—the fool, the fraud, the knave—
    That endless vigil kept
And through each brain on hands of pain
    Another's terror crept.

Alas! it is a fearful thing
    To feel another's guilt!
For, right, within, the Sword of Sin
    Pierced to its poisoned hilt,
And as molten lead were the tears we shed

For the blood we had not spilt.

The warders with their shoes of felt
    Crept by each padlocked door,
And peeped and saw, with eyes of awe,
    Grey figures on the floor,
And wondered why men knelt to pray
    Who never prayed before.

All through the night we knelt and prayed,
    Mad mourners of a corse!
The troubled plumes of midnight shook
    The plumes upon a hearse:
The bitter wine upon a sponge
    Was the savour of Remorse.

The grey cock crew, the red cock crew,
    But never came the day:
And crooked shapes of Terror crouched,
    In the corners where we lay:
And each evil sprite that walks by night
    Before us seemed to play.

They glided past, they glided fast,
    Like travellers through a mist:
They mocked the moon in a rigadoon
    Of delicate turn and twist,
And with formal pace and loathsome grace
    The phantoms kept their tryst.

With mop and mow, we saw them go,
    Slim shadows hand in hand:
About, about, in ghostly rout
    They trod a saraband:
And the damned grotesques made arabesque
    Like the wind upon the sand!

With the pirouettes of marionettes,
    They tripped on pointed tread:
But with flutes of Fear they filled the ear,
    As their grisly masque they led,
And loud they sang, and long they sang,
    For they sang to wake the dead.

"Oho!" they cried. "The world is wide,
    But fettered limbs go lame!
And once, or twice, to throw the dice
    Is a gentlemanly game,
But he does not win who plays with Sin
    In the secret House of Shame."

No things of air these antics were,
    That frolicked with such glee:
To men whose lives were held in gyves,
    And whose feet might not go free,
Ah! wounds of Christ! they were living things,
    Most terrible to see.

Around, around, they waltzed and wound;
    Some wheeled in smirking pairs;
With the mincing step of a demirep
    Some sidled up the stairs;
And with subtle sneer, and fawning leer,
    Each helped us at our prayers.

The morning wind began to moan,
    But still the night went on:
Though its giant loom the web of gloom
    Crept till each thread was spun:
And, as we prayed, we grew afraid
    Of the Justice of the Sun.

The moaning wind went wandering round
    The weeping prison-wall:
Till like a wheel of turning steel
    We felt the minutes crawl:
O moaning wind! what had we done
    To have such a seneschal?

At last I saw the shadowed bars,
    Like a lattice wrought in lead
Move right across the whitewashed wall
    That faced my three-plank bed,
And I knew that somewhere in the world
    God's dreadful dawn was red.

At six o'clock we cleaned our cells,
    At seven all was still,
But the sough and swing of a mighty wing
    The prison seemed to fill,
For the Lord of Death with icy breath
    Had entered in to kill.

He did not pass in purple pomp,
    Nor ride a moon-white steed.
Three yards of cord and a sliding board
    Are all the gallows' need:
So with rope of shame the Herald came
    To do the secret deed.

We were as men who through a fen
    Of filthy darkness grope:
We did not dare to breathe a prayer,
    Or to give our anguish scope:
Something was dead in each of us,
    And what was dead was Hope.

For Man's grim Justice goes its way,

And will not swerve aside:
It slays the weak, it slays the strong,
	It has a deadly stride:
With iron heel it slays the strong,
	The monstrous parricide!

We waited for the stroke of eight:
	Each tongue was thick with thirst:
For the stroke of eight is the stroke of Fate
	That makes a man accursed,
And Fate will use a running noose
	For the best man and the worst.

We had no other thing to do,
	Save to wait for the sign to come:
So, like things of stone in a valley lone,
	Quiet we sat and dumb:
But each man's heart beat thick and quick,
	Like a madman on a drum!

With sudden shock the prison-clock
	Smote on the shivering air,
And from all the gaol rose up a wail
	Of impotent despair,
Like the sound that frightened marshes hear
	From some leper in his lair.

And as one sees most fearful things
	In the crystal of a dream,
We saw the greasy hempen rope
	Hooked to the blackened beam,
And heard the prayer the 'hangman's snare
	Strangled into a scream.

And all the woe that moved him so
	That he gave that bitter cry,

And the wild regrets, and the bloody sweats,
    None knew so well as I:
For he who lives more lives than one
    More deaths than one must die.

IV

There is no chapel on the day
    On which they hang a man:
The Chaplain's heart is far too sick-,
    Or his face is far too wan,
Or there is that written in his eyes
    Which none should look upon.

So they kept us close till nigh on noon,
    And then they rang the bell,
And the warders with their jingling keys
    Opened each listening cell,
And down the iron stair we tramped,
    Each from his separate Hell.

Out into God's sweet air we went,
    But not in wonted way,
For this man's face was white with fear,
    And that man's face was grey,
And I never saw sad men who looked
    So wistfully at the day.

I never saw sad men who looked
    With such a wistful eye
Upon that little tent of blue
    We prisoners called the sky,
And at every happy cloud that passed
    In such strange freedom by.

But there were those amongst us all

Who walked with downcast head,
And knew that, had each got his due,
They should have died instead:
He had but killed a thing that lived,
Whilst they had killed the dead.

For he who sins a second time
Wakes a dead soul to pain,
And draws it from its spotted shroud,
And makes it bleed again,
And makes it bleed great gouts of blood,
And makes it bleed in vain!

Like ape or clown, in monstrous garb
With crooked arrows starred,
Silently we went round and round
The slippery asphalt yard;
Silently we went round and round,
And no man spoke a word.

Silently we went round and round,
And through each hollow mind
The Memory of dreadful things
Rushed like a dreadful wind,
And Horror stalked before each man,
And terror crept behind.

The warders strutted up and down,
And watched their herd of brutes,
Their uniforms were spick and span,
And they wore their Sunday suits,
But we knew the work they had been
By the quicklime on their boots.

For where a grave had opened wide,
There was no grave at all:

Only a stretch of mud and sand
    By the hideous prison-wall,
And a little heap of burning lime,
    That the man should have his pall.

For he has a pall, this wretched man,
    Such as few men can claim:
Deep down below a prison-yard,
    Naked for greater shame,
He lies, with fetters on each foot,
    Wrapt in a sheet of flame!

And all the while the burning lime
    Eats flesh and bone away,
It eats the brittle bone by night,
    And the soft flesh by day,
It eats the flesh and bone by turns,
    But it eats the heart alway.

For three long years they will not sow
    Or root or seedling there:
For three long years the unblessed spot
    Will sterile be and bare,
And look upon the wondering sky
    With unreproachful stare.

They think a murderer's heart would taint
    Each simple seed they sow.
It is not true! God's kindly earth
    Is kindlier than men know,
And the red rose would but blow more red,
    The white rose whiter blow.

Out of his mouth a red, red rose!
    Out of his heart a white!
For who can say by what strange way,

Christ brings His will to light,
Since the barren staff the pilgrim bore
    Bloomed in the great Pope's sight?

But neither milk-white rose nor red
    May bloom in prison-air;
The shard, the pebble, and the flint,
    Are what they give us there:
For flowers have been known to heal
    A common man's despair.

So never will wine-red rose or white,
    Petal by petal, fall
On that stretch of mud and sand that
    By the hideous prison-wall,
To tell the men who tramp the yard
    That God's Son died for all.

Yet though the hideous prison-wall
    Still hems him round and round,
And a spirit may not walk by night
    That is with fetters bound,
And a spirit may but weep that lies
    In such unholy ground,

He is at peace—this wretched man—
    At peace, or will be soon:
There is no thing to make him mad,
    Nor does Terror walk at noon,
For the lampless Earth in which he lies
    Has neither Sun nor Moon.

They hanged him as a beast is hanged:
    They did not even toll
A requiem that might have brought
    Rest to his startled soul,

But hurriedly they took him out,
　　And hid him in a hole.

The warders stripped him of his clothes,
　　And gave him to the flies:
They mocked the swollen purple throat,
　　And the stark and staring eyes:
And with laughter loud they heaped the shroud
　　In which the convict lies.

The Chaplain would not kneel to pray
　　By his dishonored grave:
Nor mark it with that blessed Cross
　　That Christ for sinners gave
Because the man was one of those
　　Whom Christ came down to save.

Yet all is well; he has but passed
　　To Life's appointed bourne:
And alien tears will fill for him
　　Pity's long-broken urn,
For his mourners will be outcast men,
　　And outcasts always mourn.

V

I know not whether Laws be right,
　　Or whether Laws be wrong;
All that we know who lie in jail
　　Is that the wall is strong;
And that each day is like a year,
　　A year whose days are long.

But this I know, that every Law
　　That men have made for Man,
Since first Man took his brother's life,

160

And the sad world began,
But straws the wheat and saves the chaff
    With a most evil fan.

This too I know—and wise it were
    If each could know the same—
That every prison that men build
    Is built with bricks of shame,
And bound with bars lest Christ should see
    How men their brothers maim.

With bars they blur the gracious moon,
    And blind the goodly sun:
And they do well to hide their Hell,
    For in it things are done
That Son of God nor son of Man
    Ever should look upon!

The vilest deeds like poison weeds,
    Bloom well in prison-air;
It is only what is good in Man
    That wastes and withers there:
Pale Anguish keeps the heavy gate,
    And the Warder is Despair.

For they starve the little frightened child
    Till it weeps both night and day:
And they scourge the weak, and flog the fool,
    And gibe the old and grey,
And some grow mad, and all grow bad,
    And none a word may say.

Each narrow cell in which we dwell
    Is a foul and dark latrine,
And the fetid breath of living Death
    Chokes up each grated screen,

And all, but Lust, is turned to dust
    In humanity's machine.

The brackish water that we drink
    Creens with a loathsome slime,
And the bitter bread they weigh in scales
    Is full of chalk and lime,
And Sleep will not lie down, but walks
    Wild-eyed, and cries to Time.

But though lean Hunger and green Thirst
    Like asp with adder fight,
We have little care of prison fare,
    For what chills and kills outright
Is that every stone one lifts by day
    Becomes one's heart by night.

With midnight always in one's heart,
    And twilight in one's cell,
We turn the crank, or tear the rope,
    Each in his separate Hell,
And the silence is more awful far
    Than the sound of a brazen bell.

And never a human voice comes near
    To speak a gentle word:
And the eye that watches through the door
    Is pitiless and hard:
And by all forgot, we rot and rot,
    With soul and body marred.

And thus we rust Life's iron chain
    Degraded and alone:
And some men curse, and some men weep,
    And some men make no moan:
But God's eternal Laws are kind

And break the heart of stone.

And every human heart that breaks,
    In prison-cell or yard,
Is as that broken box that gave
    Its treasure to the Lord,
And filled the unclean leper's house
    With the scent of costliest nard.

Ah! happy they whose hearts can break
And peace of pardon win!
How else may man make straight his plan
    And cleanse his soul from Sin!
How else but through a broken heart
    May Lord Christ enter in?

And he of the swollen purple throat
    And the stark and staring eyes,
Waits for the holy hands that took
    The thief to Paradise;
And a broken and a contrite heart
    The Lord will not despise.

The man in red who reads the Law
    Gave him three weeks of life,
Three little weeks in which to heal
    His soul of his soul's strife,
And cleanse from every blot of blood
    The hand that held the knife.

And with tears of blood he cleansed the
hand,
    The hand that held the steel:
For only blood can wipe out blood,
    And only tears can heal:
And the crimson stain that was of Cain

Became Christ's snow-white seal.

VI

In Reading jail by Reading town
　　There is a pit of shame,
And in it lies a wretched man
　　Eaten by teeth of flame,
In a burning winding-sheet he lies,
　　And his grave has got no name.

And there, till Christ call forth the dead,
　　In silence let him lie:
No need to waste the foolish tear,
　　Or heave the windy sigh:
The man had killed the thing he loved,
　　And so he had to die.

And all men kill the thing they love,
　　By all let this be heard,
Some do it with a bitter look,
　　Some with a flattering word,
The coward does it with a kiss,
　　The brave man with a sword!

Index of First Lines